"*But he was wounded for our transgressions, he was bruised for our iniquities:...*"
(Isaiah 53:5)

Break the Generation Curse Part 2

by Marilyn Hickey

Marilyn Hickey Ministries
P.O. Box 17349
Denver, Colorado 80217

Break the Generation Curse
Part 2

ISBN 1-56441-028-5

All scriptures are quoted from the *King James Version* of the Bible unless otherwise indicated.
Printed in the United States of America

CONTENTS

SECTION ONE

THE ORIGIN OF THE GENERATION CURSE

Chapter One
IN THE BEGINNING...

Robert was destined for failure. His father, notorious for prostituting women, committed suicide when Robert was the tender age of eight. When he was 14, Robert started his very own street gang that was known for its vicious crimes of violence and hate. At age 16 Robert was sentenced to two years in prison for three drive-by shootings and armed robberies. The day before he left for prison, his mother was murdered by a rival street gang seeking revenge. His stepfather was gunned down by the same gang three-and-a-half months later.

I'm sure if we examined Robert's family tree, we would discover generations of his family that either became caught up in a cycle of destructive behavior, or like Robert, were born into it. The good news is that by age 20, Robert heard the life-changing Word of the gospel and broke this pattern of behavior by accepting Christ as his personal Lord and Savior. The bad news is that there are many traits in our families—illnesses, attitudes, behavioral characteristics—that are passed down from generation to generation and few people know how to change this destructive trend.

God wants to shed light on the hidden causes of defeat in our families and root out stubborn sins and seeming impasses. As we discover the truth of God's Word and apply it to our personal lives, we will establish a tradition of blessing for our present and future generations—a life of abundance, fulfillment, and victory in Christ—for our children, our children's children, and the NEXT generation.

In the Garden

In the beginning, God created the perfect family. He created Adam and Eve and placed them in a utopic setting in the Garden of Eden with a charge to be blessed and live an abundant life:

And God blessed them, and [said] Be fruitful, and multiply, and replenish the earth, and subdue it: and have dominion over the fish of the sea, and over the fowl of the air, and over every living thing that moveth upon the earth. . . . I have given you every herb bearing seed, which is upon the face of all the earth, and every tree, . . . to you it shall be for meat. And to every beast of the earth, and to every fowl

of the air, and to every thing that creepeth upon the earth,
wherein there is life, I have given every green herb for
meat: . . . (Genesis 1:28-30).

Adam and Eve walked in the fullness of God's provision until Satan deceived them and they lost their dominion over the earth. Prior to their fall, their family was blessed. After the fall, however, the curse of sin, death, and destruction entered, and the family as God originally created it has not been the same since.

Because of their transgression, Adam and Eve placed themselves under a curse that not only impacted their family, but all of the families that have come after them. God pronounced a curse upon the serpent and the land. Adam was sentenced to a life of hard labor, and Eve's pain during childbearing was greatly increased. Adam and Eve went from a place of great abundance, prosperity, and peace, to death, disease, fear and every other undesirable, hereditary trait which seems to "run in the family." Adam and Eve are directly responsible for what is known today as the "generation curse":

To the woman he said, I will greatly increase your pains
in childbearing; with pain you will give birth to
children . . . To Adam he said, . . . Cursed is the ground
because of you; through painful toil you will eat of it all
the days of your life. It will produce thorns and thistles for
you, and you will eat the plants of the field. By the
sweat of your brow you will eat your food . . .
(Genesis 3:16-18 NIV).

If there is anything that you and I want, it is for our families to be strong, healthy, and blessed. Yet, from the beginning, we see the destruction of the family structure. As we trace Adam and Eve's family tree, we discover that after they were evicted from the Garden, Eve gave birth to two sons, Cain and Abel. Cain became jealous of his brother, Abel, and murdered him (Genesis 4:5,8). Cain's descendant, Lamech, followed in his forefather's footsteps and also murdered a man (Genesis 4:23). What do we see happening here? We see a definite hereditary trait that is being passed from one generation to the other.

Sins Revisited

In Exodus 20:5 we discover a profound truth having to do with these hereditary traits or family weaknesses that are passed from generation to generation:

> *Thou shalt not bow down thyself to them* [idols], *nor serve them: for I the LORD thy God am a jealous God,* **visiting the iniquity of the fathers** *upon the children unto the third and fourth generation of them that hate me.*

I'm sure all of us can think of certain families that have been ripped apart by such tendencies as alcoholism, obesity, teenage pregnancy and the like. You may be able to examine your own family tree and recognize a pattern of disease and/or infirmity. Or you may see a certain characteristic such as adultery or child abuse and think, "Wow, my family tree is a mess." Don't panic! God has made a provision for you and your future generations.

Isaiah 53:12 says that Jesus bore our sins. I don't know why, but I've always lumped sin, iniquity, and transgression together as though they were one and the same. The Bible doesn't lump them together, however. Not only did Jesus bear our sins on Calvary, but he also bore our transgressions and iniquities:

> *. . . he was wounded for our transgressions, he was bruised for our iniquities: the chastisement of our peace was upon him; and with his stripes we are healed* (Isaiah 53:5).

Sin, in the context of Isaiah 53:12, means "to miss the mark." So if and when you sin, you miss the mark or fall below the mark of what God has called you to do. We all have been guilty of "missing the mark" at some time or another: *"For all have sinned, and come short of the glory of God"* (Romans 3:23). That's why Jesus had to go to the Cross, to carry the burden of our sins.

Transgression, on the other hand, means to "trespass," or "overstep preestablished boundaries." We can trespass against man and God. If I were to come up to you and purposely step on your foot, or violate your "NO TRESPASSING" sign by entering onto your property without permission, I'd be transgressing against you.

You may say, "Oh, I have been hurt by people." Well, Jesus was wounded for those trespasses, and you don't have to carry them any more. He took the wounds for you. Isn't that dynamite? You may say, "Marilyn, I have wounded people. I have trespassed against people and it is hard for me to think that I could be forgiven." Regardless of what you've done or think, the Bible says that Jesus was wounded for your trespasses. He has taken the wounds of those things that you have done to others and that others have done to you. All you have to do is repent and let Him have them!

If you look at the body of Christ, you'll see seven places where Jesus' blood was shed: He was circumcised; His beard was plucked; they pressed the crown of thorns on His head; His hands, feet, and side were pierced; and His back was beaten. I find this interesting because seven is the number of completion. I believe God is telling us that Jesus has completely provided for every kind of weakness, infirmity, and sin that we could have through the seven wounds He endured. We can truly say Christ's provision is full and complete.

The Mystery of Iniquity

Now let us take a look at the word, *iniquity*, which means "to bend" or "to distort (the heart)." It also implies "a certain weakness or predisposition toward a certain sin." Isaiah says Christ was "bruised for our iniquities" (53:5 KJV).

If you commit a certain sin once and repent of it and never do it again, then that's the end of it. However, your sin becomes an iniquity when you keep committing that same act; it goes from being a sin to an iniquity, something that is practiced over and over again until it becomes spontaneous. Given certain circumstances or the "right" environment, you will "bend" in that direction.

If a sin is repeatedly committed, it becomes an iniquity which can be passed down through the bloodline. When a person continually transgresses the law, iniquity is created in him and that iniquity is passed to his children. The offspring will have a weakness to the same kind of sin. Each generation adds to the overall iniquity, further weakening the resistance of the next generation to sin.

Exodus 20:5 speaks very specifically about the iniquities of the forefathers. If the family tree is not cleansed of this iniquity, then each generation becomes worse and will do what their parents, grandparents, and great grandparents did! The next generation will bend in the same way of the past generations, and it becomes a bond of iniquity or generation curse in that family.

We have all seen families where one or both parents or grandparents were alcoholics and one or more of the offspring became alcoholics too. And to think, it all started as a sin with that one person who overindulged; but because they practiced it and did not try to get free through godly repentance, their drinking became an iniquity. Consequently, that family begins to bend or has a predisposition toward alcoholism.

My father had two nervous breakdowns. I didn't know this until later, but my grandfather and great grandfather had mental and emotional problems too. I never thought of that as being an inherited trait or something that I had a predisposition toward.

When I was 36 years old, however, I was under tremendous pressure. The devil spoke to me and said, "You are just like your father. You look and act like him. You are going to have a nervous breakdown."

Although I shouldn't have, I began to entertain that thought. One day I felt like I was at my breaking point. Again the devil spoke to me and said, "You're just like your father and you're going to have a nervous breakdown!"

I foolishly agreed, "Yes, I'm just like my father. I'm going to have a nervous breakdown." It was at that point that the Lord spoke to me and said, "That's right! You are just like your Father! I'm your Father and I've never had a nervous breakdown, and neither will you!"

Hallelujah! Jesus was bruised for my iniquities! His work on the Cross was the provision I needed to change the tide of a generation curse and walk in total mental health and victory! He's done the same for you, too, through the wounds and bruises He endured on the Cross—the provision has been made to restore you and your family to that state of blessedness Adam and Eve once enjoyed in the Garden.

The difference between a wound and a bruise is that if you wound yourself, it will eventually scab over and heal. A bruise, however, can stay around for a long time. It may become discolored and can even go so deeply as to bruise the bone. An iniquity can be likened to a bruise because it stays around and goes to the bone from generation . . . to generation . . . to generation.

The Apostle Paul had a revelation of this when he wrote II Thessalonians:

> For the mystery of iniquity doth already work: . . .
> (II Thessalonians 2:7).

The "mystery of iniquity" Paul is referring to is the unseen and mysterious connection between a father's sins and the path of his children. For example, if the father is a liar and thief, his children are prone to the same behavior, regardless of their training, social, cultural, or environmental influences.[1]

Both sin and iniquity are spiritual terms. We don't always grasp the significance of such terms as we would for something relating to the natural. Paul wrote that the things not seen are understood by the things which are made (see Romans 1:20). He was referring to the natural universe—creation—when he spoke of the things that are "made." Likewise, the spiritual can be understood by the natural; for example, diabetes as well as cancer can be an inherited disease.[2]

The Law of Generation

Everything produces after its own kind. Within every seed there is the inherent ability to reproduce itself. Jesus Himself used this law of generation in the Sermon on the Mount when He said:

> Beware of false prophets, which come to you in sheep's clothing, but inwardly they are ravening wolves. Ye shall know them by their fruits. Do men gather grapes of thorns, or figs of thistles? Even so every good tree bringeth forth good fruit; but a corrupt tree bringeth forth evil fruit (Matthew 7:15-17).

"What," you might ask, "produces bad fruit?" In the natural, we know that if the fruit is malformed or the tree is not bearing fruit according to its stock, then a mutation has taken place. The same is true in breeding animals. If the offspring are not true to the breed, the breeders usually "eliminate" them from their pool of animals. Mutants are not wanted. They are a corruption of the line of animals being bred.

As illustrated in the creation of the earth in Genesis 1, everything reproduces after its own kind. We acknowledge this principle in buying a pedigreed animal, but we completely ignore this principle when we deal with people.

When you go to a medical doctor for a physical examination or because you have a medical problem, he will usually take a medical history before he begins his diagnosis and treatment. What you tell him of your past problems, and the problems your parents, grandparents, and siblings may have an affect on what he may look for or what tests he may order. Many diseases are genetic or inherent in a family line and are inherited from one or both parents. These disorders may be in some or all of the offspring, or may skip a generation or two and occur in the grandchildren or great grandchildren.[3]

Healthy couples who have healthy ancestors almost always have healthy offspring. This is the law of generation set in motion in Genesis 1: "everything reproduces after its own kind." Genetic inheritance is a natural counterpart to spiritual inheritance. Understanding natural laws concerning genetic inheritance gives us a working model for the principle of spiritual inheritance. The Bible gives examples of spiritual laws and their workings in the lives of various characters and their descendants.[4]

We took a look at Adam and his lineage in the early part of this chapter, so let's take a look at Noah, a man who was "... *perfect in his generations, and ... walked with God"* (Genesis 6:9).

Though Noah was considered "perfect," there were still some flaws in the bloodline of Noah and his sons; Ham especially was affected by the curse of iniquity. When Noah became drunk, he lost control of his son Ham. The weakness to sin caused him to give way to temptation, and the Bible says that Noah was "uncovered" in his tent. The Hebrew word for *uncovered* is used in Leviticus many times, primarily in regard to sexual sins involving incest.

It is highly unlikely that it was a simple case of nudity. The curse that Noah pronounced on Canaan was too drastic for such a trivial thing as that. When we regard God's displeasure with homosexuality, we see that He judged this sin very severely.

Scripture will bear out that this was indeed the case with Ham. The Amorites were descendants of Canaan, who in turn descended from Ham. They were in the land of Canaan, which is the land that the Israelites were to take by force from the Amorites. These were the people who were worshiping all manner of idols and false gods and their worship was characterized by gross sexual perversions and orgies.[5]

The Amorites' Iniquity

In Genesis 15 we read that God gave assurance to Abram that he would inherit the land of promise because his descendants would go into a strange land for 400 years, but after four generations they would return because *". . . the iniquity of the Amorites is not yet full"* (Genesis 15:16).

If you recall in Genesis 13, Abram and Lot separated and Lot chose the plain where the cities of Sodom and Gomorrah were located. The inhabitants of these cities were also Canaanites. Like the Canaanites, they practiced homosexuality and their cities were destroyed because of it.

Abraham negotiated with God for Sodom and Gomorrah but only righteous Lot and his family were spared. Because the rest of the inhabitants were totally corrupted, they were annihilated. At that time, the iniquity of the Sodomites and the Gomorrahites was full:

> *And Abraham drew near, and said, Wilt thou also destroy the righteous with the wicked? Peradventure there be fifty righteous within the city: wilt thou also destroy and not spare the place for the fifty righteous that are therein? And the LORD said, If I find . . . fifty righteous within the city, then I will spare all the place for their sakes . . . Peradventure ten shall be found there. And he said, I will not destroy it for ten's sake* (Genesis 18:23,24,26,32).

The mystery of iniquity had already come to pass: the sins of the fathers had been passed to the third and fourth generations of the inhabitants of Sodom and Gomorrah (Exodus 20:5). By three or four generations of successive and cumulative iniquity, the children were so crooked and perverse that there was no possibility that they would ever walk upright before the Lord. By four generations, their spiritual bloodline was completely corrupted and defiled. Their hearts were inclined only to evil. It was in reference to the Canaanites that God said to Israel in Deuteronomy 20:16,17:

> But of the cities of these people, which the LORD thy God doth give thee for an inheritance, thou shalt save alive nothing that breatheth: But thou shalt utterly destroy them; . . . .

God's command to Israel was to kill everything that was alive—people and animals; to kill everything that could harbor spirits (the New Testament gives evidence that animals can harbor spirits):

> And there was there an herd of many swine feeding on the mountain: and they besought him that he would suffer them to enter into them. And he suffered them. Then went the devils out of the man, and entered into the swine: and the herd ran violently down a steep place into the lake, and were choked (Luke 8:32,33).

The iniquity of the Canaanites was so entrenched that they had to be completely eliminated from the face of the earth in order to destroy their bloodline. To allow them to remain would have subjected Israel to the possibility of becoming contaminated with the same iniquity, and that iniquity would have no doubt spread throughout the nation.

Israel, however, got into serious trouble when they failed to execute God's judgments. Neglecting to eliminate the Canaanites allowed iniquity to multiply and when the land fell to iniquity, God brought the sword and purified the land. Ezekiel 8 and 9 give a vivid picture of God having to cleanse the bloodline. In Ezekiel 8 we see the charge God had against Israel—idolatry with its attendant deterioration of moral and social disciplines. And in chapter 9, angels were sent through the city to slay everyone who didn't have the "mark" of God on his forehead:

> And to the others he said in mine hearing, Go ye after him through the city, and smite: let not your eye spare, neither have ye pity: Slay utterly old and young, both maids, and little children, and women: but come not near any man

upon whom is the mark; and begin at my sanctuary. Then
they began at the ancient men which were before the house.
And he said unto them, Defile the house, and fill the courts
with the slain: go ye forth. And they went forth, and slew
in the city (Ezekiel 9:5-7).

Ezekiel recoiled in anguish at the slaughter and feared that none would be left of the Israelites. God's response to him was that He was doing what was necessary to cleanse the bloodline:

Then said he unto me, The iniquity of the house of Israel
and Judah is exceeding great, and the land is full of blood,
and the city full of perverseness: for they say, The LORD
hath forsaken the earth, and the LORD seeth not. And as
for me also, mine eye shall not spare, neither will I have
pity, but I will recompense their way upon their head
(Ezekiel 9:9,10).

God assured the prophet that all would be well because in the end, after the judgments had fallen and the only ones left would be righteous, the generations that would come from them would be righteous and serve the Lord (see Ezekiel 14:22,23).[6]

Iniquity, like sin, must be dealt with. People in both the Old and New Testaments understood this and traced their sins back to their forefathers. In Daniel 9:16, Daniel talks about the iniquity of "our" fathers. In Psalms 51:5, David said, *"Behold, I was shapen in iniquity; and in sin did my mother conceive me."* It wasn't the sexual act that was sin, because God created the sexual union for people to reproduce and to have a good, physical life together. What David is saying by inspiration of the Holy Spirit is, "I inherited the iniquity of my fathers, and through conception, their weaknesses have been passed down to me."

You've heard the expression, "You're just like your Aunt So-and-so"? Well, Lamentations 5:7 says, *"Our fathers have sinned and are not; and we have borne their iniquities."* In other words, Aunt So-and-so is dead, but you are carrying her iniquity or that same predisposition to sin.

As I mentioned earlier, I've seen certain behavioral characteristics in my family from time to time that I know are inherited from my parents and grandparents. I recognize them as iniquities, but I've come to realize that I don't have to live under a generation curse—and neither do you! Jesus, our Kinsman Redeemer, was bruised for our iniquities, thereby making it possible for us and our children to inherit family blessings.

Chapter Two
SIN OR INIQUITY?

In Chapter 1, we looked at iniquities that are passed from generation to generation. We saw how certain hereditary traits—such as child abuse, alcoholism, and obesity which seem to "run in the family"—originated from just one person who practiced a certain sin until it became a lifestyle or stronghold in that family tree. Once entrenched, the sin became an iniquity—a weakness, bend, or predisposition toward a certain behavior. As that person continually yielded to the temptation of that sin, the demonic forces that influenced him gained dominance in his soulish realm where the mind, will, and emotions are located, and began to control that individual and, subsequently, his future generations!

This phenomena is known as a family iniquity or generation curse. If you search the Scriptures, however, you will quickly discover that a family is not the only thing that can be dominated by a generation iniquity; nations, the priesthood (church leadership), and the land can also inherit a curse.

Land Iniquities

Second Samuel 21 says there was a famine in the land for three years. David went to God in prayer: "God," he said, "something is wrong because You have promised us abundance. Is there something spiritually wrong that is holding back Your blessings?" God said, "Yes. It's because of the sins of Saul that he committed against the Gibeonites. Their blood cries, 'Vengeance,' from the ground to Me."

When David asked the Gibeonites what kind of retaliation he should pay, they asked that seven of Saul's sons and grandsons die for what their grandfather had done. The Gibeonites hung Saul's seven descendants. Rizpah interceded so that her sons would have a decent burial. David buried her sons with Saul and Jonathan. After the land was cleansed with blood, the famine ended.

Some years ago, a man wrote to me and told me about his farmland; a certain kind of weed came up every year, which poisoned the cattle if they ate it. He said that it was all over his area and they would have to pay for crop dusters to spray the land every year. It was very expensive and aggravating.

One day he heard that his land might be cursed. His grandfather had bought the land from the Indians and some underhanded things may have been done to them, so the Indians put a curse upon it. The man and his wife began to pray—there was an iniquity upon their land. They fasted and prayed and drove around the land and repented of the iniquities of their fathers and grandfathers. They applied the blood of Jesus to cleanse the land.

The next year the weeds came up. When their son pulled up one, they discovered that the root system was drying up; those few weeds that did come up were withered at the roots. They haven't had that problem since. The curse on their land was broken by repentance, acknowledging the sin, and applying the blood of Jesus.

As we saw in the Garden of Eden, the curse entered the world when Adam and Eve transgressed. God pronounced a curse on them, the land, and their future generations. (See Genesis 3:16-19.) Since God's original command to Adam and Eve was to "be fruitful, multiply, and replenish the earth," the nations and leadership that came out of Adam's loins were made subject to the effects of their fall as well.

National Iniquity

Ah sinful nation, a people laden with iniquity, a seed of evildoers, children that are corrupters: they have forsaken the LORD, they have provoked the Holy One of Israel unto anger, they are gone away backward (Isaiah 1:4).

A national iniquity is a sin such as genocide, abortion, or idolatry in which a nation as a whole is involved. For example, abortion, political and religious corruption, and pornography are just a few of the national iniquities that plague the United States.

The wisest man who ever lived, Solomon, began a national iniquity in the nation of Israel that eventually led to its downfall:

But king Solomon loved many strange women, together with the daughter of Pharaoh, women of the Moabites, Ammonites, Edomites, Zidonians, and Hittites; Of the nations concerning which the LORD said unto the children of Israel, Ye shall not go in to them, neither shall they come in unto you: for surely they will turn your heart after their gods: . . . And he had seven hundred wives, princesses, and three hundred concubines: . . . For it came to pass, when Solomon was old, that his wives turned away his heart after other gods: . . . (I Kings 11:1-4).

How tragic! Because of his inordinate appetite for what the Bible terms "strange" women, Solomon's heart was turned from worshiping the true and living God to idolatry: the worship of the creature instead of the Creator. In reading the Bible you will note that throughout the pages of the Old Testament, God warns Israel repeatedly not to intermingle with the people from the other nations. This was not because God was selfish and wanted the Israelites all to Himself, but because God understood the "mystery of iniquity," that the sins of the fathers are passed onto the third and fourth generations—even nations!

First Corinthians 5:6 says, "*. . . a little yeast works through the whole batch of dough*" (NIV). As Solomon practiced idolatry, his sin became an iniquity and was inherited by his son, Rehoboam, his grandson, Abijam, and last but not least, the nation of Israel. The entire bloodline had been corrupted:

*And Rehoboam the son of Solomon reigned in Judah. . . . And Judah did evil in the sight of the LORD, and they provoked him to jealousy with their sins which they had committed, above all that their **fathers had done.** For they also built them high places, and images, and groves, on every high hill, and under every green tree. Now in the eighteenth year of king Jeroboam the son of Nebat reigned Abijam over Judah. And **he walked in all the sins of his father, which he had done before him:** . . .* (I Kings 14:21-23; 15:1,3).

Like family iniquity, national iniquity will take dominion and infect every citizen. Frankly, I think the conflict in the former Yugoslavia is a family iniquity turned national that has never been resolved or cleansed.

Psalms 119:133 says, "*Order my steps in thy word: and let not any iniquity have dominion over me.*" The psalmist was crying out for God to prevent any individual, family, or national iniquity from dominating him. He wanted to be free! We know God is faithful, and that He has provided a way of escape from all iniquities through the shed blood of His Son, Jesus. One of the first steps to individual, family, or national cleansing is to confess that family or national iniquity:

> *If we confess our sins, he is faithful and just to forgive us of our sins, and to **cleanse** us from all unrighteousness* (I John 1:9).

National Cleansing

The Bible is our roadmap or blueprint for every situation we may ever encounter. The same holds true for families and nations. By examining Biblical examples of how the nation of Israel was set free of its national iniquity, you will see how to cleanse your family of iniquity. In Daniel 9, Daniel goes into a time of fasting and prayer. He confesses the sins of his fathers and includes himself in it. He prayed and fasted for 21 days:

> *...O Lord, the great and dreadful God, keeping the covenant and mercy to them that love him, and to them that keep his commandments; **We have sinned, and have committed iniquity,** and have done wickedly, and have rebelled, even by departing from thy precepts and from thy judgments* (Daniel 9:4,5).

When I look at Daniel, I think, "Daniel didn't sin, his fathers did." The Bible says Daniel was a very godly man who prayed three times a day. He received the revelation of King Nebuchadnezzar's dream, and was delivered by God from the lion's den.

Daniel was highly esteemed by God. He was called "Beloved of the Lord." Why did he include himself as being guilty of the national iniquity? Because he understood the "mystery of iniquity"—the sins of the fathers passed to future generations. He knew that Israel's 70-year captivity was almost over. God had told them through Jeremiah, that at the end of 70 years they would return to Jerusalem, rebuild the Temple, and He would restore their land. The 70 years were almost over and there were no signs that their captivity was ending. Why? Because the iniquity of the nation had not been confessed and the bloodline cleansed.

Daniel said, "We have committed iniquities." In other words, he knew he was a part of the iniquities that held them in bondage. Because he confessed the sins of the nation's forefathers, there was a turnaround for the nation of Israel. If you remember, at that time they were under Babylonian captivity. But after Daniel prayed, God moved and brought in the Medes and the Persians. They diverted the Euphrates River, came under the wall, and took the city. The new king, Cyrus, signed a decree and said that the Jews could return to Jerusalem to rebuild their Temple and their nation. But this didn't happen until *after* Daniel had confessed his and Israel's national iniquity in prayer.

Sometimes we have to look back through our family's tree; we may say, "My grandparents and father had temper tantrums, and I do too. God forgive them, wherever and however these tantrums began, forgive them and forgive me. Cleanse our family tree with the blood of Jesus!" That is when the curse is broken!

Nehemiah is another example of someone who repented for the nation. He was burdened because he knew the Temple had been rebuilt but the walls of the Temple were down. He knew that as long as they were down, the Israelites would not live in Jerusalem. He interceded to God on Israel's behalf:

> . . . *I beseech thee, O LORD God of heaven, the great and terrible God, that keepeth covenant and mercy for them that love him and observe his commandments: Let thine ear now be attentive, and thine eyes open, that thou mayest hear the prayer of thy servant, which I pray before thee now, day and night, for the children of Israel thy servants, and confess the sins of the children of Israel, which we have sinned against thee: both **I and my father's house have sinned** (Nehemiah 1:5,6).*

Nehemiah confessed the sins of his fathers. "Oh, God," he pleaded, "have mercy on us!" Nehemiah could have said, "I didn't do anything wrong! I don't have to confess the things that they did." But he recognized the mystery of iniquity at work in his bloodline and realized he had the same bend his fathers and the nation of Israel were guilty of: "God forgive us for our national sins and what we have done! We are guilty! Forgive us and cleanse us with the blood!"

After Nehemiah's prayer, the king of Persia let him go back to rebuild the walls and the gates and made provision for building supplies. They finished building in 52 days, and the most prosperous time that Israel had was the next 400 years. Why? Because if you cover your sins or the sins of your family, you will not prosper:

> He that covereth his sins shall not prosper: but whoso confesseth and forsaketh them shall have mercy (Proverbs 28:13).

BUT, if you confess your sins, you will prosper. Nehemiah didn't try to cover or deny his family/national iniquities. Likewise, we need to humble ourselves and pray over the sins that have been committed in America. We need to include ourselves, because that's when healing can come.

In Nehemiah 9, the entire congregation repented for their iniquities. God healed their land and cleansed them:

> If my people, which are called by my name, shall humble themselves, and pray, and seek my face, and turn from their wicked ways; then will I hear from heaven, and will forgive their sin, and will heal their land (II Chronicles 7:14).

This is a very simple remedy to iniquity. Confess the iniquity and take the cleansing of the blood. Jesus was bruised for our iniquities. He carried our sins. He was wounded for our transgressions and by His wounds we are healed. But without His wounds we, and our nation, are still sick!

Peter saw this when Simon, who appeared to be saved, asked to buy the gift of the laying on of hands for people to receive the baptism of the Holy Spirit:

> And when Simon saw that through laying on of the apostles' hands the Holy Ghost was given, he offered them money, Saying, Give me also this power, that on whomsoever I lay hands, he may receive the Holy Ghost. But Peter said unto him, Thy money perish with thee, because thou hast thought that the gift of God may be purchased with money. For I perceive that thou art in the gall of bitterness, and in the bond of iniquity (Acts 8:18,19,23).

Peter said, "I see that you are in the bond of iniquity. You still have the iniquity of greed holding on to you." Simon repented and asked Peter to pray for him because he did not want to be bound by greed. Sometimes an iniquity can hold on to you; confess it and take the cleansing of the blood and be set free.

Family Iniquity

Jesus talked about a corrupt tree and a good tree, and how to prune a tree. The ax has to be put at the root in order for your family tree to bring forth good fruit. God has never wanted an evil or corrupt tree. He's always wanted a good tree.

If you study the families of the Old Testament, you will find that God had divine destinies for them. The family names were important, as well as their geographic locations. Even the type of food each family produced was divinely purposed by God.

Consequently, when a family gets into sin, it can avert the plan God has for it. Remember when we looked at iniquity, we saw that it is a practiced sin that becomes a bend in that person's heart. The devil has a plan for your family—a plan of sin. Because iniquity can be passed to the next generation, it can destroy God's divine destiny for that family and the devil's destiny will come forth.

Jacob's Wrestling Match

When Jacob wrestled with the angel in Genesis 32, the angel asked him, "... *What is thy name?* ... " (vs. 27). That question was embarrassing to Jacob because he had been practicing the same sin and trespass over and over again. Even his name, which means, *supplanter,* speaks of a person who is not to be trusted. He was a conniver, schemer, and deceiver.

Jacob answered the angel, "Oh, I'm Jacob." He hated to say it, but when he admitted he was of questionable, moral character, then the angel said, "Your name is no longer Jacob, it's *Israel,* 'Prince of God.'" From this example, we see that the only way to get free of sin, trespass, and iniquity is to confess it. It is only then that God can turn you, your family, or your nation from a "Jacob" into an "Israel."

Jeremiah 14:20 says, *"We acknowledge, O LORD, our wickedness, and the iniquity of our fathers: for we have sinned against thee."* When I read this scripture, I realized that God prospers His people when they confess not only their iniquities, but the iniquities of their fathers.

None of us like to think that what we do has an effect upon our children. We like to feel independent about our actions and assume that our attitudes and behavior only affect us. However, Exodus 20:5 assures us that our iniquities will be passed on to our children, our grandchildren, and even nations!

Achan's Transgression

When the Israelites entered the Promised Land, they were told not to take any spoils from the battle of Jericho. Achan, disobeyed, however, and stole a Babylonian garment, 200 shekels of silver, and a wedge of gold and hid them. When the Israelites fought their next battle, no one knew what Achan had done and they lost the battle.

God told Joshua that there was sin in the camp and Joshua called the people to repent. Through Joshua, God gave Achan the opportunity to repent and stop what happened to him and his family, but he didn't. As a result, Achan and his entire family were stoned:

> And Joshua, and all Israel with him, took Achan the son
> of Zerah, and the silver, and the garment, and the wedge
> of gold, and his sons, and his daughters, and his oxen, and
> his asses, and his sheep, and his tent, and all that he had:
> and they brought them unto the valley of Achor. . . . And
> all Israel stoned him with stones, and burned them with fire,
> after they had stoned them with stones (Joshua 7:24,25).

The sin of Achan was visited upon the children. That was a great tragedy but it is a picture of what II Thessalonians 2:7 refers to as the "mystery of iniquity" which is in operation from generation to generation. Had they not been killed, that "bend" toward covetousness in their family, would have been passed down to future generations and may have grievously affected the nation of Israel. Repentance and cleansing of the blood would have changed this.

Priestly Iniquity

Korah rebelled against the leadership of Moses and Aaron. If you go back and study the family tree of Korah, you'll see he was assigned to be the worship leader for the Tabernacle. His family tree was to produce worship and praise and was a part of the priestly family that took care of the Tabernacle. God had a divine assignment for his family, but Korah decided he was more spiritual than Moses and Aaron and that they shouldn't be leaders.

"We should be the leaders," he said. He began to plant seeds of rebellion and caused others to rebel against Moses and Aaron. Moses didn't retaliate; he prayed instead. After he prayed, God opened the ground and swallowed Korah:

> And it came to pass, as he [Moses] had made an end of speaking all these words, that the ground clave asunder that was under them: And the earth opened her mouth, and swallowed them up, and their houses, and all the men that appertained unto Korah, and all their goods (Numbers 16:31,32).

What a shame! Korah's family tree and destiny was swallowed up because his pride and rebellion became an iniquity. However, not all of Korah's family tree was destroyed. His sons did not stand with him in his rebellion. They decided that just because their father was following the path of iniquity, it didn't mean they *had to* follow suit. They were not into ancestor worship.

Because Korah's sons chose not to stand with their father, they were not swallowed up by the earth. If you follow their lineage, you'll see that his descendants became worship leaders in David's Tabernacle and in Solomon's Temple, which was one of the seven wonders of the ancient world.

As you read the Bible, you will read again and again about the sons of Korah—from generation to generation they are leading worship. Psalms 42 was written by one of the sons of Korah, and we are aware of at least eight other psalms that were written by them.

Korah's sons sought after righteousness and did not yield corrupt fruit. They made a decision to be godly and to follow God's divine destiny for them. The devil would have destroyed that family with iniquity. Although Korah didn't repent of his rebellion, his sons did and they were free to fulfill what God had planned for them.

Saul and his son Jonathan are another example of a family tree where the father was corrupt but the son chose not to follow that path of family iniquity. When Saul came after David with great anger and jealousy trying to kill him, Jonathan protected him. That is really something because that iniquity in Saul could have been passed to Jonathan.

If you remember the story, Saul and Jonathan both died in battle. But because Jonathan had entered into a covenant with David, a family blessing had been established. After David assumed his kingship, he enquired about Jonathan's seed because he wanted to bless his family line. David tracked down Jonathan's lame son Mephibosheth and restored the lands that had been Saul's and allowed him to eat at the king's table every day.

"Why," you ask, "did David bless Mephibosheth?" Because of the covenant relationship he had with his father, Jonathan. When you sow good seed in the kingdom, you begin a generation blessing. Instead of Jonathan choosing the iniquity of his father, he chose the blessings of God and his next generation reaped the benefits.

Jonathan understood that David was anointed by God to be king. He didn't look in the natural, he looked at the supernatural. Had Jonathan dwelt on the natural way of doing things, he could have become jealous and enraged like his father. After all, the law of natural inheritance says that the first-born son would inherit his father's throne. Jonathan, however, chose God's way, consequently establishing a family tree of good fruit, which was passed on to his future generations.

The Sons of Aaron

Aaron had four sons, two of whom got drunk and offered strange incense before the Lord. The fire of God devoured them. God told Aaron not to mourn their deaths because what they did was wrong. Their iniquity could have destroyed the Aaronic priesthood. Aaron's two other sons were godly, and the Aaronic priesthood as a whole was good. They did not get into iniquity because Aaron accepted God's reasons for destroying his sons.

Eli, the priest, did just the opposite. God had warned Eli about his sons' behaviors. They were not only whoremongers, but they were desecrating the offerings the people were bringing to God and defiling Him in their eyes. Eli failed to do anything about it, so when their iniquity "was full," God cut off Eli's bloodline. God's divine destiny for them was the priesthood, but their iniquity destroyed them.

Like national curses, a priestly curse must be broken through repentance. Because Eli didn't repent, the iniquity went from generation to generation and finally destroyed Eli's entire family tree. Eventually, God destroys iniquity because it gets worse with each generation. The way to break a curse is to acknowledge the iniquity, repent, and accept the blood.

Chapter Three

TRACING THE ROOT SYSTEM OF YOUR FAMILY TREE

The foundation of every plant or tree is its root system. If you examine the roots of some plants, you'll notice that the initial roots are almost microscopic. As the plant continues to grow, however, the roots become thicker and darker until over a period of time, depending on the type of plant, they could become thick enough for you to swing on.

The same is true for the family tree and family iniquities. The problem you or a loved one may be experiencing right now in the area of anger, depression, or some other iniquity that has gotten a hold on your family, originated at the beginning of your family's root system—generations ago—with great, great, great grandfather, who had a tendency to "sin."

Way Down Deep

The iniquities of your forefathers are often like evil seeds that are planted deep within the soil of your soul (mind, will, and emotions). Sometimes they are planted within you before you are born. Other seeds are planted through your early childhood experiences. Some seeds may remain dormant and never sprout. Others, given the right environment, sprout and become strong trees that produce evil or undesirable fruit.

When you act upon and nurture these weaknesses or bends inherited from your family tree, the seeds often become overwhelming, full grown trees producing fruit of controlling and compelling evil in your life.

What is the source of the evil seed? Jesus gives us the parable of the wheat and the tares in Matthew 13. He likens the kingdom of heaven to a man who sows good seed in a field, but *the enemy* sows tares or evil seeds among the good. What Jesus is telling us is that the children of God coexist with the children of the devil until the Son of man sends His angels to separate the two. From this we understand that the devil is the one who plants evil seed. Generation curses are another work of his.

Once you understand who is behind the evil work that is being passed from one generation to the next, you will come to realize that the most effective way to kill a generation curse is to cut the tree at its roots—

below the surface of the ground. If you can cut the roots and destroy them, the tree will die. Otherwise, the iniquity, like any vegetation, will sprout leaves once again.

What are the roots to the evil tree? Where did they come from? How are they destroyed? John the Baptist had the answer to this question when he said:[7]

> And now also the axe is laid unto the root of the trees: every tree therefore which bringeth not forth good fruit is hewn down, and cast into the fire (Luke 3:9).

You will find the roots to your family tree's iniquities in the sins and iniquities of your forefathers. This may be difficult for some people to accept because of their love for their family. I love my family, too, but I don't love them enough to be enslaved by their iniquities.

What's That Odor Coming Out of Your Closet?

The evil tree represents the bond of iniquity that you may find in your life. The fruit on the tree represents habitual sins—iniquities. These are areas of repeated failure and spoiled fruit.[8] Some evil fruit exists whether you have participated in it or not. For example, you may have homosexual tendencies, but have never acted upon them.

It's time to bring those hidden sins and iniquities out of the closet and to the forefront. To uncover the root system of your family tree, you must begin with your parents. Draw a diagram of a tree similar to the one on page 43. Begin with your father. Ask yourself, "What sins, habits, or failures do I know of in my father's life?" If you have problems looking at your dad from this perspective, remember that your purpose is not to condemn or expose him, but to correct some problems in your life by getting at the root of the curse or iniquity you've inherited.

Make a list of his sins and iniquities. Then ask yourself the same question about your father's parents, listing these traits as well. After you cover the father's side of the family, then examine your mother's side of the family in the same manner. Again, it is important to look at the sins and the iniquities of the forefathers in relation to the fruit on the tree. As the sins and iniquities of the forefathers are listed, you may discover additional areas of iniquities in your own life.

Even if you are adopted or don't know anything about your parents or grandparents, just list the generation curses that you are aware of in your own life. You can believe, however, that these characteristics had their beginnings in the sins of your forefathers. After the diagram of your tree is completed, one of two things will happen: you will either be amazed by the reality of the evil tree and its significance, or, the overall picture may trigger the need to put additional fruit on the tree.

Spoiled Fruit

You may discover that there are a number of generation iniquities at work in your personal life as well as your family's. Some specific curses include: sterility (Deuteronomy 28:18); divorce and adultery (Deuteronomy 28:30); rebellion or loss of your children (Deuteronomy 28:32); debt (Deuteronomy 28:44). Even your home or property could be under a curse (Deuteronomy 28:38-42).

There are also physical curses that are passed down in the bloodline. Disease often develops as a direct result of sin in a person's life. Some research, for example, has linked arthritis, kidney and gallbladder problems to the sin of bitterness and unforgiveness.

You can also be cursed by the words someone speaks over you. Commonly known as word curses, these are curses that anyone in authority speaks over the life of another. This could include parents, grandparents, physicians, teachers, and even religious leaders such as pastors. Word curses such as, "You're so stupid," attack the very soul of an individual and can be inherited by the next generation.[9]

Symbolism and Types of Generation Curses

Symbolism has been used historically in both the Bible and literature to give the reader a "picture" or mental image of a person, place, or thing. It has been proven that if you can visualize or form a mental picture of something, then you are more likely to remember it.

Throughout the Bible, God uses animals as symbols. When God gave dreams to the prophets of old, many times those dreams were a picture language to them.

Jesus is depicted throughout the Bible as the Lion of the tribe of Judah. Unlike the devil, who walks about "as a roaring lion seeking whom he may devour," Jesus is the real king of the jungle. Scripture refers to Him as King of kings, and Lord of lords.

My husband, Wally, and I recently returned from Zimbabwe, Africa. We noticed that the people in that part of Africa had what they called "totems." These totems are symbols of their tribes. For example, there was one tribe that had a totem of a snake. The snake had its own house on a long stick, and is kept in the back yard of every family in that tribe. The tribal belief is that at night, their god—the snake—leaves the totem and returns before day light.

The snake in the Bible and in America is anything but a god. I'm sure that when many of you think about the nature of a snake, you think of a sneaky, crafty, slimy creature. But in some African countries, they won't as much as eat a snake because they consider it a deity. They say that the nature or spirit of that snake comes into them.

Basil Frasure in his book, HOW TO DESTROY THE EVIL TREE, gives us a long list of unclean animals, which are symbolic of the uncleanness or iniquities that enter into a family tree and is passed from generation to generation.

The Lizard

The lizard is a fearful animal. It moves quickly and jumps at the slightest movement or noise; it is afraid of everything. I know people who are like that—they are so filled with fear that they will flee at the drop of a hat.

Some of my family members are like this. I believe there is an iniquity of fear upon my family. Many of them are fearful of what could happen, what the future holds, or what if something went wrong and they lost everything they've worked so hard to obtain. I've seen it in my parents, grandparents, myself, and my children.

Needless to say, I don't like that. To have a fear of God is one thing, but when you see fear surfacing in each generation, it becomes a phobia that says your circumstances and the devil are bigger than God. Do you feel like fear is an iniquity in your family? Would you say that if there were a totem or family logo in your back yard, it would be that of a lizard?

Blind as a Bat

You've heard the expression, "They only come out at night"? That is very true of bats, and the reason is these nocturnal creatures are blind.

Many families live in spiritual darkness. No matter what you tell them, how hard or often you witness to them, they just *cannot* see the light of God's Word. Even in the midst of a crisis that would bring most families to their knees, a family that is blind to spiritual things will be oblivious to what is going on. It's almost like there is an invisible wall that keeps them dwelling in darkness. No wonder Paul said:

> . . . *Hearing ye shall hear, and shall not understand; and seeing ye shall see, and not perceive: For **the heart of this people is waxed gross,** and their ears are dull of hearing, **and their eyes have they closed;** lest they should see with their eyes, and hear with their ears, and understand with their heart, and should be converted, and I should heal them* (Acts 28:26,27).

The word, *gross*, in this context means "to thicken or render callous." In other words, the spiritual blindness began when someone in the bloodline rejected the gospel of truth and hardened his heart to the things of God. This led to spiritual blindness and an iniquity which is passed from generation to generation.

I remember the husband of a friend of ours and how blind he was to spiritual things. You could take him to the most anointed church service and he'd never get anything out of it. Jesus Himself could have talked to the man and not gotten through to him. It was almost as though the gospel was beyond his natural comprehension. His father and grandfather were the same way.

Because of their heart condition, this family will remain in darkness until someone in their family tree comes into the saving knowledge of the Lord Jesus Christ. The devil works in darkness. But when the Light comes, the darkness is dispelled and the devil is revealed for who he is—a defeated foe and lying wonder. Psalms 119:130 says, *"The entrance of thy words giveth light; it giveth understanding unto the simple."* Once the power of darkness is broken over a family, they can be set free of spiritual blindness.

The Snake

The snake has always been a symbol of lying and deception. From Genesis to Revelation, Satan is depicted as a liar and deceiver. As a matter of fact, his first appearance in the Bible was in Genesis, when he deceived Adam and Eve in the Garden of Eden. In a family tree, the snake is symbolic of the destructive tendencies of lying and deception.

Racial and ethnic prejudice is a deception that has become an iniquity in families and nations. Many wars have been and are being fought along racial and ethnic lines. When I was just six years-old, I overheard my grandparents make a racial comment. I dearly adored them, but when I heard their comment something inside of me said, "This is wrong." They began to call me a name which implied that I had a love for the people they were slandering.

They were being deceived by the devil because of their own racial prejudice. That deception was passed to their children and grandchildren. Thank God it was not passed to me. I chose not to follow that same pattern of family iniquity.

The Owl

The owl has been used as a symbol of wisdom and knowledge. I can remember our local library used to encourage us to read and the owl was the symbol on the bookmarks they'd give us. The owl in a family tree represents false knowledge.

The first recorded sin as found in Scripture was that of a seeking of knowledge. Eve was tempted to eat of the tree of knowledge of good and evil. The serpent told her that if she would eat of the tree that she'd become as gods, knowing good and evil:

> *And the serpent said unto the woman, Ye shall not surely die: For God doth know that in the day ye eat thereof, then your eyes shall be opened, and ye shall be as gods, knowing*

good and evil. And when the woman saw that the tree was good for food, and that it was pleasant to the eyes, and a tree to be desired to make one wise, she took of the fruit thereof, and did eat, and gave also unto her husband with her; and he did eat (Genesis 3:4-6).

I know a young lady who was raised in Satanism. She was dedicated to Satan as a child, and her head was filled with false knowledge about him. When her mother and brother became born again, they started bringing her to church. She'd sit in the service as though a dark cloud was over her head. She had the look of death on her.

Even though she'd get headaches each time she attended service, she continued coming until one night, the light of God's Word penetrated the darkness that had this woman bound. Today she is one of the most radiant Christians in our church. She was set free from the occult and the false knowledge that Satan is god.

The Vulture

The vulture is an unclean bird. We associate the vulture with dead animals. We know that by nature, it eats creatures that have already died and begun to decay. This bird is shown in the death scenes of a lot of the old western films. It could be seen circling in the air, hovering over its dying victim, waiting to descend so it could eat its flesh.

In a family tree, the vulture is a symbol of tendencies that are associated with death. These tendencies include both suicidal or homicidal predispositions.

Suicide and murder have become common occurrences in today's society. I'm sure you've either heard of or perhaps lived in communities where suicide or violence seemed to run in certain families. I've heard of a family in which the mother overdosed on pills, her son committed murder, and the grandson committed a murder/suicide. You say, "How tragic!" I agree. But this is just one of the many iniquities that can be found in a family tree.

The Frog

The frog is symbolic of carnal or sexual sin in a family tree. In nature, frogs are known for their multiplication and jumping. Some people are just like frogs—they jump into situations without thinking, and some even jump from bed to bed.

With the HIV virus and the threat of AIDS being at an all time high, I'm sure many of you would agree that sexual sin runs rampant throughout the world. Pornography, homosexuality, and pedophilia (having sex with children), has almost become common place. This iniquity has become so entrenched in the fabric of American society, that both the American family and the nation are affected by it.

Sexual iniquity in a family tree is a real strong sin to deal with because it literally enslaves the members of each generation:

Know ye not, that to whom ye yield yourselves servants to obey, his servants ye are to whom ye obey; whether of sin unto death, or of obedience unto righteousness? (Romans 6:16).

. . . know ye not that he which is joined to an harlot is one body? for two, saith he, shall be one flesh. . . . Every sin that a man doeth is without the body; but he that committeth fornication sinneth against his own body (I Corinthians 6:16,18).

The Egyptians were very much into sexual sin. Some of the animals they worshiped had to do with the types of sexual sins they committed. (In a sense they were like the African village that had totems in their back yards.) God judged the Egyptians with the plagues he sent to destroy them. Many family trees are completely wiped out because of their sexual sin. This does not have to happen to your family tree, however; God has provided a way of escape through repentance, forgiveness, and the shed blood of Jesus.

The Spider

The spider is known for the webs it spins. No matter how well you clean your house, you'll find a spider in some remote corner of your home. If you get rid of the web but don't destroy the spider, it will spin a web in another spot in your home. Spiders are very territorial. With each web they communicate, "This turf is mine, and I'm not going to share it." One of the strongest and most dangerous webs that a man can weave is possessiveness. The spider in the web in a family tree is symbolic of greed, selfishness, and jealousy.

The Bible says that the *"love of money"* is the root of all evil (see I Timothy 6:10). Greed, selfishness, and jealousy piggy-back off one another. Greed breeds selfish behavior, "I want it all to myself and refuse to share with anyone else. There's only enough for me!" Once greed and selfishness team up with one another, then jealousy kicks in. "You have more than me, and I want what you have too."

America is full of greed. We're not a team-oriented society; everything is "Me, me, me, me." Greed is a strong, inherited trait in most family trees because success and material well-being are equated with money. To most people, it doesn't matter how you make your money, just as long as you have a lot of it.

Many a family has been destroyed because of this iniquity. And like the spider and her web, this family trait cannot be eradicated by simply destroying the web (the symptom); the spider (the root) must be destroyed as well. Otherwise, it will go to another part of your home—the next generation of your family tree—and spin an even bigger, stronger web.

The Scorpion

The scorpion is a creature that inflicts great pain. It is symbolic of a tendency toward pain. This tendency in a family tree could be in the form of self-pity.

There are many people who have a tendency to dwell upon the emotional hurts and pain of their past. They have a "Woe is me," attitude, and get great comfort out of licking their wounds. If you attempt to tell them that Isaiah 53:4 says Jesus has already born their griefs and carried their sorrows, they will become upset with you. After all, "You can't possibly understand how bad they've been hurt and are still hurting!"

Many Christians are living with emotional pain from their past—

some in ignorance and some by choice. The good news is Christ won their freedom over 2,000 years ago and by His stripes, they are free!

The Hornet

Hornets also inflict pain, but they are better known for their anger and aggressive attacks. In a family tree, they are symbolic of anger, rage, bitterness, and revenge.

People who have this kind of iniquity in their family tree, are likely to become angry at the drop of a hat. They are very negative people who are either always angry at someone or always looking for someone else to hate. They have very few friends. You can see the anger raging from generation to generation.

The Turtle

Are you as slow as a turtle? This animal is considered by many as one of the slowest moving animals God made. It sticks its head in its shell when trouble comes. Some families are like turtles: they get very little accomplished. They often shirk responsibility when they need to assert themselves. The turtle symbolizes both laziness and procrastination in a family tree.

These unclean creatures are representative of tendencies toward sin that you may find in your life or in your family tree.

Prayer of Confession

By now I'm sure you're beginning to understand that we all have inherited certain family iniquities. I'm sure you're also beginning to realize that you and your future generations can be free to walk in the blessings you've inherited from Jesus through His death, burial, and resurrection. Say this prayer out loud:

Father, I confess that I have iniquities. I thank You, today, that when I confess my sins, then You are faithful and just to forgive me. I repent of my iniquities. I not only repent of my sins and iniquities, but I also repent and ask You to forgive my parents and grandparents for what they did. I also forgive them; I am not holding it against them. I take

*the cleansing of the blood. I bind the devil and cast him
out of my family tree. In Jesus' name, amen.*
Through the finished work of Jesus Christ, you have the authority
to declare that the generation curses in your family are broken!

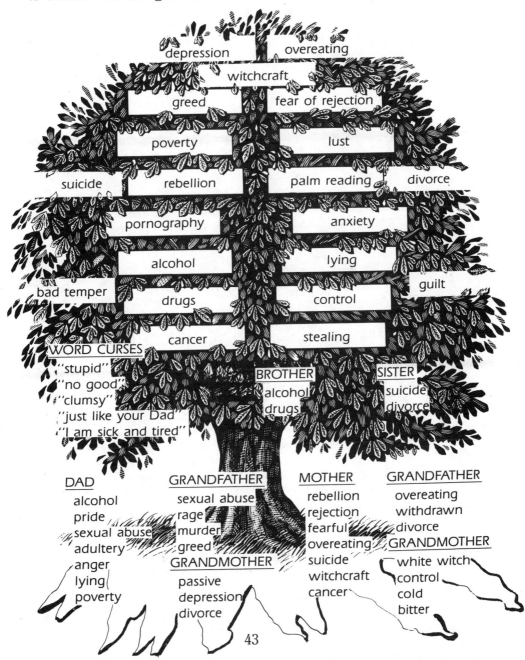

SECTION TWO

JESUS REVERSED THE CURSE

Chapter Four

THE BELIEVER'S COVENANT: REDEEMED FROM THE CURSE

Sin is never *fair*, but it is predictable. Sins that are repeatedly committed are like weeds planted in the heart. You can mow them down, but until they are understood and dealt with, they will crop back up. Iniquities are like the seeds of weeds—they may die, as your forefathers have—but they will return the next year or in this case, the next generation. Whether they are planted by you, your parents, or your forefathers, the result is a crop of inherited weaknesses or family iniquities:

> *As the bird by wandering, as the swallow by flying, so **the curse causeless shall not come*** (Proverbs 26:2).

> *Thou shalt not bow down thyself to them, nor serve them: for I the LORD thy God am a jealous God, **visiting the iniquity of the fathers upon the children unto the third and fourth generations of them that hate me*** (Exodus 20:5).

The law of iniquity states that the sins of the fathers will continue to the third and fourth generation for those who hate God. What about you and me who love God? For us, God has made a provision to reverse the curse of iniquities. Just as iniquities are passed through the bloodline, your exemption from the law of iniquity is through blood, the blood sacrifice of your covenant with God. In the Old Covenant that sacrifice was of bulls and goats but in the New Covenant the perfect, precious blood of Jesus cleansed you from sin and iniquity.

You no longer have to live bound by iniquities and generation curses and be defeated by sin because Jesus became both your "sin offering" and the "scapegoat" for your iniquities. His physical body was sacrificed and His perfect blood was offered to God for your sins and iniquities. He took your iniquities and buried them in the sea of forgetfulness. You have something better than the "types" and "shadows" of the Old Testament; you have a better covenant in Jesus:

> *In the same way, after the supper he took the cup, saying, This cup is the **new covenant in my blood,** which is poured out for you* (Luke 22:20 NIV).

47

Jesus took on Himself the curse of your iniquity. He became cursed so that you could be set free and blessed:

> Christ hath redeemed us from the curse of the law, being made a curse for us: for it is written, Cursed is every one that hangeth on a tree (Galatians 3:13).

Your Magna Carta

Your Emancipation Proclamation, the document of your freedom and deliverance from generation curses and iniquities is found in Isaiah 53:5,11:

> But he was wounded for our transgressions, **he was bruised for our iniquities:** the chastisement of our peace was upon him; and with his stripes we are healed. He [God] shall see the travail of his soul, and shall be satisfied: by his knowledge shall my righteous servant [Jesus] justify many; **for he shall bear their iniquities.**

Why was Jesus "bruised" for your iniquities? Because your iniquities, inherent weaknesses, are like bruises. As we've already seen, natural bruises leave a discoloration. They usually hurt the most when you first get them, then they become discolored. Bruises can go very deep, even to the bone. Heart bruises—iniquities—can begin with a crisis such as death, abuse, or trauma that begins a sin pattern which is passed on to the next generation. Unlike broken bones that can be set or a wound that can be sown up, bruises can't be treated. A medical doctor will tell you to live with the bruise and it will eventually go away.

What the doctor means is that your body will repair itself. Your blood provides nourishment to the body's cells and takes away the waste. Just as your natural blood brings health to areas that are bruised and removes waste, the blood of Jesus is required to heal your heart bruises and carry away your iniquities. Bruises of the heart don't heal by themselves and go away, you must apply the blood of Christ for complete recovery.

Maybe a better example is what happens to a piece of fruit that gets bruised. If you drop an apple, a bruise is created. In fact, when an apple is bruised it discolors, begins to rot, and eventually the entire apple spoils. Without the help of Jesus, the bruises you receive from your iniquities, if not dealt with, will cause you to rot and affect your entire life. Jesus, however, bore your bruises—your iniquities:

The Spirit of the Lord is upon me, because He hath anointed me to preach the gospel to the poor; he hath sent me to heal the brokenhearted, to preach deliverance to the captives, and recovering of sight to the blind, **to set at liberty them that are bruised** (Luke 4:18).

Physical Afflictions and Generation Iniquities

Doctors are aware that physical afflictions can be a result of a generation iniquity. When you show signs of certain types of diseases, they want to know if you have a family history of that disease. Maybe arthritis, diabetes, or heart problems run in your family.

I was only 23 years old when the doctor told me: "You have an enlarged heart; there's *nothing* you can do about it." The doctor's words tore away at my faith. Immediately the devil reminded me that my father had a heart attack, and now the same thing was going to happen to me.

I'm sure that the devil held his breath as he waited to see how I would respond to his lie. I was a young Christian at that time, but I knew enough of God's Word to stand in faith for physical healing. While it was true that my dad did have a heart attack, I knew that Jesus had come to replace family iniquities with blessings and to set me free from every life-threatening sickness.

My husband prayed with me, and we stood on the promises found in Isaiah 53:5 and Psalms 103:3,4:

. . . the chastisement of our peace was upon him; and with his stripes we are healed (Isaiah 53:5).

Who forgiveth all thine iniquities; who healeth all thy diseases (Psalms 103:3,4).

That same year I was miraculously healed of an enlarged heart! Just recently I had my yearly checkup; the doctor said, "Your heart is excellent." Praise the Lord; God reversed the curse that Satan tried to pass down to me from my father. I have a "fixed" heart. You don't have to live under physical curses because Christ has redeemed you from the curse.

Old Covenant Believer

One of the best examples of a person delivered from a family iniquity is Rahab. Rahab lived in Jericho and was the Canaanite prostitute who hid and saved the lives of the two spies Joshua had sent to look over the city. God had judged the Canaanites; their sins were so terrible that He was going to exterminate them. Rahab was condemned to die; but, instead, she became a believer when she confessed Jehovah as the one true God:

> . . . *for the LORD your God, he is God in heaven above, and in earth beneath* (Joshua 2:11).

Rahab asked the spies to spare her and her family. The spies told her to hang a scarlet cord from her window. The Israelites marched around the city for seven days and on the seventh day God performed a miracle by smashing down the city's walls.

This wonderful story doesn't end here. Because of Rahab's faith-filled actions, she reversed the curse in her family tree and started a heritage of blessings. Rahab married one of the Israelites. She and her husband had a son named Boaz, who married Ruth. Ruth and Boaz had a son named Obed, whose name means "worshiper." Obed had a son named Jesse, who had a son named David. Jesus, as a descendant of David, is also from the family of Rahab.

God is no respecter of persons; what He did for this prostitute of a cursed people, He wants very much to do for you. He has provided a way for you to be free from the *law of iniquity* operating in your life. The curse of iniquity in your family tree has been reversed through the New Covenant that was cut for you by Jesus' shed blood. You have a choice, you can live under the curse of family iniquities passed on through your blood, or through the blood of Jesus receive the blessing. The blood can bless or curse.

Roots of Iniquity

The roots of iniquity are pulled up through the blood of Jesus.

Isaiah 53 says that Jesus "bore" our sin, He was "wounded" for our trespasses, and "bruised" for our iniquities. The blood of Jesus is all sufficient, powerful, and devastating to family iniquities in your bloodline. To be effective, however, the blood of Jesus must be applied to your situation. Positive thinking, psychological counseling, even doing "religious" things like singing in the choir, while good will not solve the problem. They may provide temporary relief, but only the blood of Jesus is the permanent answer—transforming your curse into a blessing.

If you haven't already done so, turn back to the last pages of Chapter 3 and take the opportunity to repent, apply the blood, and experience the witness of the Holy Spirit to your total release and complete freedom. The blood of Jesus has purchased your freedom from iniquity and the witness of the Holy Spirit applies the anointing that breaks the yoke—freeing you of the shackles of your family iniquities:

> *And it shall come to pass in that day, that his burden shall be taken away from off thy shoulder, and his yoke from off thy neck,* **and the yoke shall be destroyed because of the anointing** *(Isaiah 10:27).*

Types and Shadows

The Old Testament is full of "types and shadows" of things to come. To really understand the provisions of the New Covenant, we need to understand what God provided for Old Testament believers. He has made a way for His people to have freedom from generation iniquities.

The Jewish ceremony of the Day of Atonement gives us a picture of redemption. Through this ceremony you can see how Jesus purchased your freedom from iniquities. When this ceremony was reenacted in heaven on your behalf, Jesus became your High Priest and blood sacrifice.

Picture with me the most important day of the Jewish year, the tenth day of the seventh month, Tishri—the Day of Atonement. On that day the sins, trespasses, and iniquities of the people were cleansed. On the eve of the Day of Atonement, the people fasted and humbled themselves and repented. The next morning they gathered before the gates of the outer court in solemn assembly.

While the hushed crowd waited outside the Temple grounds, inside the high priest, having already selected two goats, seven rams, and a bull, began the ceremony by washing (purifying) himself and dressing in the holy, linen robes of his office. All but one of the animals, a goat, would be sacrificed. The high priest offered blood sacrifices for the *atonement*, which means, "reconciliation of the guilt by divine sacrifice," for the sanctuary, tabernacle, brazen altar, and his fellow priests.

Then he killed the goat of the sin offering, for the sins, trespasses, and iniquities of all the people of Israel. The blood from the goat chosen to be the *sin offering* was sprinkled on the Mercy Seat for the sins of the people. (The Mercy Seat was the place where the presence of God dwelt—the golden center area on the lid of the Ark of the Covenant located between the two Cherubim.)

The high priest placed both hands upon the head of the remaining goat, the scapegoat, and confessed over it all the sins, transgressions, and iniquities of the people. Then the scapegoat was removed and taken into the wilderness. God had accepted the blood of the goat sacrifice as a sin offering and cleansed them of all their sins, and removed their iniquities. Likewise, the blood of Jesus has cleansed you and your family tree of generation iniquities:

> And the goat shall bear upon him all their iniquities unto a land not inhabited: and he shall let go the goat in the wilderness (Leviticus 16:22).

Heroine of the Old Covenant

I believe, on one such Day of Atonement, waiting for cleansing from iniquities with the others, was a young woman named Jehosheba. She was the bride of a young priest, and the daughter and granddaughter of two of the most evil and wicked women in the Bible—Jezebel and Athalia. Jehosheba had possibly the worst family tree of anyone in the Bible; yet God, even in Old Testament times, redeemed her from the iniquities of her family.

Omri, Jehosheba's great-grandfather, was a "bad" king of the

Northern Kingdom called Israel. He was a shrewd politician and sought to make peace with the nation of Zidon, by marrying his son to Jezebel, who became the wife of Ahab. Jezebel introduced the nation of Israel to the worship of Baal—the most despicable, demon religion of that day.

The prophet Elijah opposed Ahab and Jezebel and caused a drought in the land. After three years Elijah faced down the prophets of Baal by calling down fire to consume his sacrifice to God. He then ended the drought. Elijah also prophesied a curse upon Ahab and Jezebel and their descendants. He told them their family would be extinguished.

That was only the beginning of the bad news for Jehosheba. In an attempt to bring peace between the Northern and Southern kingdoms, the "good" king of Judah, Jehosphaphat, accepted a marriage between his son and the daughter of Jezebel, Athalia. Like her mother, Athalia introduced the worship of Baal to her husband and the Southern Kingdom of Judah. After her husband died in battle, his son, Ahaziah, became king and after a few years he was killed.

Athalia saw her son's death as an opportunity to take the throne of Judah and sent assassins to murder her grandchildren. She believed that she could gain the throne of Judah by eliminating all her son's heirs. What a grandmother! She became the only woman to reign over either the Northern or Southern kingdoms. Had she succeeded in killing all of her grandchildren, the seed of David would have ended and there would have been no Messiah because Jesus had to come through the seed of David.

When Jehosheba heard what her mother was doing, she slipped into the nursery and saved the youngest child from the assassin's blade. She and her husband guarded the child until he was seven-years old. Then her husband brought him to the Temple to be crowned king and Athalia was killed.

Jehosheba became one of the little-known heroines of the Bible despite her family tree. God doesn't care how rotten your family tree is. When you receive His cleansing, your family iniquities are broken! If God could deliver Jehosheba under the Old Covenant just think what He can do through a new and better covenant for you, your children, and the next generation.

If you are concerned about your family, because unlike Jehosheba, your mate isn't a priest or even a believer yet, and you see family iniquities operating in your home, then take heart. It only takes one believing mate to sanctify a house. If you are that one believing person in your home, it's enough. You can end the generation curse and establish the blessing for your family tree:

> *For the unbelieving husband is sanctified by the wife, and the unbelieving wife is sanctified by the husband: else were your children unclean; but now are they holy* (I Corinthians 7:14).

The Curse Reversed

Before I was saved and Spirit-filled, I attended a Sunday school class and everything the teacher said, I challenged. It's rather embarrassing now to recall some of the ridiculous things I said then. I certainly never mentioned them to my daughter, Sarah.

When Sarah was a junior at Oral Roberts University, she spent a summer in Germany at a university. When she returned to the U.S. she told me that she wasn't sure that she believed in Jesus. My heart went down to my feet as I listened to her say some of the very things I had said so long ago in that Sunday school room. Sarah was raised in a Spirit-filled home, brought up on the Word of God, and had received the Lord at an early age.

The Lord spoke to me and said, "Don't fall apart, be cool!" So I told her, "The enemy is trying to steal your faith but Jesus will make Himself real to you." Needless to say, my husband, Wally, and I prayed. What was happening here? An iniquity that I had started was operating in my daughter.

After returning to ORU, Sarah called me one night. She had recommitted her life to the Lord. When I asked her how it happened, she told me about a young man at school with whom she was studying. He had experienced a similar loss of faith while studying at Harvard. His father insisted that he attend ORU for a year; and, consequently, he regained the truth of his salvation. This young man, having himself just returned to the Lord, led her back to the truth.

Coincidence? No, God had reversed the curse and had begun the blessing, and He will do the same thing in your life and for your next generation.

Chapter Five

THE REWARDS OF YOUR REDEMPTION

Man was created with a desire and need for an intimate relationship with God. There is a place in everyone that craves a Father-son or Father-daughter relationship with his or her Creator. Until that void is filled and the desire satisfied by a relationship with Him, human beings will hunt for the answer, trying various substitutes to satisfy their desires. Mankind is out of balance and incomplete without a personal relationship with God.

I remember the first time I heard of a child divorcing his parents. I was aghast at the idea. Yet when Adam and Eve sinned, that was exactly what they did; they divorced their Father, God. All of us have been deeply wounded by the rejection of a loved one, but that only gives us a small glimmer of how Adam's act of sin and rebellion must have broken the heart of God. How did the One Who is defined by the word "love" feel when His children divorced Him through an act of disobedience?

What did God do? Did he become angry, pout, seek vengeance, or hide and nurse His pain? No, out of His great love for you and me, He initiated a plan made before the foundation of the world that would make it possible for *all men* to return to a relationship of intimacy with Him:

> For God so loved the world, that he gave his only begotten
> Son, that whosoever believeth in him should not perish, but
> have everlasting life (John 3:16).

Not only did man lose his relationship with God, but he brought upon himself and this world the curse of sin and sin's companion, death. When Adam and Eve chose rebellion over obedience, and sin over righteousness, they "adopted" a new father and god—Satan. They poisoned themselves and all creation with their sin. God withdrew from intimacy with man because in His goodness, God is repulsed by sin and He must judge it. Adam and Eve had made themselves an enemy of God. Sin is more than an obnoxious irritant to God, it is His enemy:

> Wherefore, as by one man sin entered into the world, and
> death by sin; and so death passed upon all men, for that
> all have sinned (Romans 5:12).

Satan must have been filled with malicious glee over his part in corrupting man. I'm sure he felt that he had won a major battle with God, because the very creatures whom God had lovingly crafted were now in the camp of the enemy. Did Satan win that day? No way:

> *He that committeth sin is of the devil; for the devil sinneth from the beginning. **For this purpose the Son of God was manifested, that he might destroy the works of the devil*** (I John 3:8).

Jesus stripped himself of His glory and humbled himself to be born as a man for the dual purpose of "destroying the works of the devil" in your life and restoring you to "sonship" with the Father. Why salvation? So you can end the curse of sin and iniquity in your life and family's and establish generation blessings:

> *For sin shall not have dominion over you: . . . ye were the servants of sin, but ye have obeyed from the heart . . . Being then made free from sin, . . . For the wages of sin is death; but the gift of God is eternal life through Jesus Christ our Lord* (Romans 6:14,17,18,23).

> *The thief cometh not, but for to steal, and to kill, and to destroy: **I am come that they might have life, and that they might have it more abundantly*** (John 10:10).

Old Things Passed Away

I think one of the saddest stories in the Bible is that of Judas, a man who remained bound by the iniquity of greed while in the presence of the One Who could release him from his iniquity. This greed caused him to betray Jesus, the Son of God. In Acts 1:18 it says:

> *Now this man* [Judas] *purchased a field with the reward of **iniquity;** and falling headlong, he burst asunder in the midst, and all his bowels gushed out.*

Judas carried the money bag because he was the treasurer of Jesus' ministry team. It's hard to imagine how someone could walk, talk, see miracles, and hear Jesus for over three years and still be bound by a family curse or an iniquity of his own making. Judas illustrates that being a "hearer of the Word" is not enough. To enter into the rewards of your redemption, you have to become a "doer" also:

Do not merely listen to the word, and so deceive yourselves.
Do what it says. Anyone who listens to the word but does
not do what it says is like a man who looks at his face in
a mirror and, after looking at himself, goes away and
immediately forgets what he looks like (James 1:22-24 NIV).

One legacy of your former life is the curse of sin that all mankind received through Adam and Eve's act of disobedience. That "state of sinfulness" was judged by God and merely awaited the execution of the sentence. Jesus took that sentence and bore the penalty of sin for you, me, and all mankind. He died in our place:

For as by one man's [Adam's] *disobedience many were made*
sinners, so by the obedience of one [Jesus] *shall many be*
made righteous (Romans 5:19).

You were delivered from your sin nature. As a sinner, sin was natural for you, but when you made Jesus the Lord of your life, your sin nature passed away, and you became "new" in Christ and now have "His nature" in you:

Therefore if any man be in Christ, he is a new creature:
old things are passed away; *behold, all things are become*
new (II Corinthians 5:17).

The domination and the power of the sin nature was defeated in your life. Where before you were obligated to sin, you now have a choice and a desire not to sin. You are free of sin's authority to live a victorious life that pleases God. Yes, it's still possible to hear the voice and give in to the temptation of sin, but sin will never be able to regain control over you. Hallelujah, you are free:

Knowing this, that our old man is crucified with him, that
the body of sin might be destroyed, that henceforth we
should not serve sin. For sin shall not have dominion over
you: . . . (Romans 6:6,14).

All Things Become New

In previous chapters we discussed that family iniquities can come in the form of anger, obesity, alcoholism, etc. These iniquities are the obstinate sins, and recurring family illnesses that are passed on through the bloodline. There is no question that Jesus, acting as your sin sacrifice and the scapegoat for iniquities, dealt the death-blow to this problem area:

> *Who gave himself for us, that he might **redeem us from all iniquity**, and purify unto himself a peculiar people, zealous of good works* (Titus 2:14).

Many Christians suffer from a "personality crisis." They know "what" they are—new creatures in Christ—but don't know "who" they are, and how their new identity relates to their victory over family iniquities:

> *I have been crucified with Christ: nevertheless I live; yet not I, but Christ liveth in me: and the life which I now live in the flesh I live by the faith of the Son of God, who loved me, and gave himself for me* (Galatians 2:20).

You are a "new creature in Christ"! According to the Greek translation of II Corinthians 5:17, God created you as a "new being who has never existed before." That means those hereditary family iniquities are no longer your heritage. You've heard the expression, "That's just not you"? Those family iniquities just aren't you anymore! You have a new birthright. As a child of God, you have a wonderful inheritance: blessings instead of curses, abundance instead of lack, and health instead of sickness:

> *. . . giving thanks to the Father, who has qualified you to share in the inheritance of the saints in the kingdom of light. For he has rescued us from the dominion of darkness and brought us into the kingdom of the Son he loves, in whom we have redemption, the forgiveness of sins* (Colossians 1:12-14 NIV).

You once were an enemy of God, but now He sees you as a son, a new person recreated in the likeness of Himself. When proud parents show off their newborn baby, people say things like: "He has his father's nose, his mother's chin," and so forth. When God looks at you, He says: "Yes, he has My righteousness, and My love, and he looks just like My Son." Every time you find the words "in Christ" in the New Testament, give it special attention because they describe what you look like to God. Hold those scriptures before you like a mirror—they are the *real* you:

> *. . . when we were God's enemies, we were reconciled to him*
> *through the death of his Son, . . .* (Romans 5:10 NIV).

> *Because those who are led by the Spirit of God are sons*
> *of God. . . . you received the Spirit of sonship. And by him*
> *we cry, 'Abba, Father'* Romans 8:14,15 NIV).

Jesus sees you as an individual member of the Body of Christ. Under His leadership, you are "more than a conqueror," victoriously overcoming every strategy of the enemy in your life. You are a citizen of His kingdom with kingdom rights and responsibilities: you have eternal life, victory over sin and Satan, the right to use the name of Jesus in prayer, the right to the indwelling of the Holy Spirit, and more:

> *No, in all these things we are more than conquerors through*
> *him who loved us* (Romans 8:37 NIV).

> *Now you are the body of Christ, and each one of you is*
> *a part of it* (I Corinthians 12:27 NIV).

God's Power In You

Have you tried and tried and yet failed to overcome your hereditary weaknesses? Then you are close to deliverance. If you have discovered that your own efforts will never be enough to secure a lasting victory, then you are ready to turn to God's power to destroy the ties—your inherent weaknesses—that bind you:

> *But as many as receive him, to them gave he* **power to**
> **become the sons of God,** *even to them that believe on his*
> *name* (John 1:12).

When you were born again, God came to live in you to restore you to the wholeness of "sonship." Having lived for years as a slave to family iniquities, you defined yourself by your weaknesses. You may have heard yourself saying things like: "I'm always sick; I go from one thing to another! I'll always be poor, too. Why, if it wasn't for bad luck, I'd have no luck at all! I've tried to give up drinking, but it's stronger than I am. I'll go to my grave doing it—just like my dad."

You can define yourself down to a pitiful, powerless creature—a victim of your own weaknesses. You are not a victim but a victor; not a loser but a winner; not on the bottom but above every sin, situation, and sickness. You can take God's Word for it because God gave you power! It's not a human power, but the God-kind of power.

You don't have to plead and beg for deliverance, the gift has already been given to you. You don't have to be worthy, go to Bible school, be called to full-time ministry, or be perfect with no past mistakes. This very minute you have within you the power of God.

This power is not just for your salvation—that was only the beginning. As a child of God, you are promised an "abundant" life:

> *. . . I am come that they might have life, and that they might have it more abundantly* (John 10:10).

God's power will roll over and crash anything—including family iniquities—that stand between you and the abundant life due to you as a son of God. It is time for you to redefine yourself by the Scriptures and assume your real identity as God's son—a supernatural being that wields the "power" to break the curse in your family tree and to establish generation blessings.

Receive Redemption

Your redemption from sin, trespasses, and iniquities were purchased once and for all by Jesus Christ through His death, burial, and resurrection. Jesus forged a New Covenant with His shed blood to free mankind from sin and death:

> *. . . Whosoever shall call on the name of the Lord shall be saved* (Acts 2:21).

Have you accepted Jesus as Lord and Savior? Have you joined the family of God? Only those who are born again can be free from generation iniquities—the negative spiritual traits that you have either begun or those passed on to you by your forefathers. Your only escape is to be born anew through the blood of Jesus and to receive God as your spiritual Father. When you become born again, your old family traits are cancelled and the qualities and blessings of Jesus become your birthright:

> *For whom he did fore know, he also did predestinate to be* **conformed to the image of his Son,** *that he might be the*

firstborn among many brethren (Romans 8:29).

Perhaps you have never received the new birth, or maybe you have grown cold in your relationship with God. Maybe family iniquities have caused you to give up and backslide:

And because iniquity shall abound, the love of many shall
wax cold (Matthew 24:12).

You can change that now. If you are sincere and want to find freedom from your family iniquities, and desire a fresh new start, pray this prayer out loud:

Dear Jesus, I believe that You died for my sins,
transgressions, and iniquities, and that You rose again on
the third day. I confess to You that I am a sinner and that
I need Your love and forgiveness. Come into my life, forgive
my sins, and give me eternal life. I confess You now as my
Lord. Thank You for my salvation! Amen.

Congratulations! Your acceptance of Jesus Christ as your Lord and Savior is the best decision that you have ever made. You have become a "new creation" in Christ. The Trinity dwells in you: God the Father, Jesus the Son, and the Holy Spirit. You are set free from sin and servitude to Satan:

Therefore if any man be in Christ, he is a new creature: . . .
(II Corinthians 5:17).

For the law of the Spirit of life in Christ Jesus hath made
me free from the law of sin and death (Romans 8:2).

Welcome to God's family! Welcome to His life!

Chapter Six

BREAKING THE PATTERN... ONCE AND FOR ALL

Not long ago we had our bushes trimmed in front of our home. Some of them were overgrown and really looked bad, so we had a man come and trim them back to stumps. We thought the man who trimmed the bushes would pick up the trimmings and haul them to the dump. However, he left them and didn't come back. So we called and left messages on his answering machine. Finally, he came back with his truck and I thought, "Good, the problem is solved." However, he didn't put the limbs and rubbish in his truck, he bound them into bundles and placed them by the curb. He said, "The trash men will pick them up." There were five or six large bundles over six feet high. I thought, "The trash haulers will take one look at all this and say, 'Forget that.'"

The next morning was our day for trash pick up, so when I left my home for work I prayed, "Lord, surround my trash with favor." When I returned home, I was so relieved to see all those bundles gone. I thought, "Thank you Lord!" Then the Lord spoke to me and said, "Marilyn, the garbage in a person's life can't be surrounded with favor; neither can I be expected to carry it off. I can't give favor to garbage or cover it over. The way to get rid of trash is by repenting of it." Then the blood of Jesus cleanses and past sins are cast into the sea of forgetfulness.

God wants you to get rid of the trash in your life. He will not overlook it or give it favor. He wants you to take the steps necessary to deal with family iniquities in your life.

The past chapters have been building to this point. In chapters 1, 2, and 3 you learned the origin of generation curses, and in chapters 4 and 5 you learned that God has made a provision for your freedom from these iniquities. Now it is time for you to get free, to take what you've learned thus far and break the pattern of your family iniquities . . . once and for all.

Acknowledge and Confess the Iniquities of Your Forefathers

If you haven't done so already, take the time now to uncover the roots of the iniquities in your family tree. Ask yourself, "What sins, habits, failures, or illnesses do I know of in the lives of my forefathers?" Deal with each person in your last four or five generations individually, starting with your father and mother. Don't be concerned if you didn't know some of your forefathers; the Holy Spirit will reveal things that are hidden to you.

This step is so vital that I suggest you stop reading and turn back to the first section of the book to the third chapter for information on how to discover "past" roots to your "present" problems. If you are a person who finds it difficult to see anything wrong in your parents, remind yourself that it is not your purpose to condemn or slander them, but to discover the roots of your problems.

To take the steps for deliverance, you need to determine as clearly as possible where the roots of the fruit you see on your tree come from. The evil fruit in your life came from somewhere. Don't forget to include physical afflictions in your inventory. Ask the Holy Spirit for help. Ask Him to reveal to you things that are hidden. As you review your legacy of iniquity, take as much time as you need and write down your findings because if you are vague and don't believe for anything in particular, then you are not going to receive anything. To get specific results, you need to pray specifically.

Perhaps it seems strange to you to confess the sins of your parents. You're probably thinking, "Marilyn, I've never heard of this before." The following scriptures are only a few of the many that deal with this subject but they will establish your heart in this almost forgotten Biblical principle:

> If they shall **confess their iniquity, and the iniquity of their fathers,** with their trespass which they trespassed against me, and that also they have walked contrary unto me; Then will I remember my covenant . . . (Leviticus 26:40,42).

> And the seed of Israel separated themselves from all strangers, and stood and **confessed their sins, and the iniquities of their fathers** (Nehemiah 9:2).

> We acknowledge, O LORD, our wickedness, and the iniquity

of our fathers: for we have sinned against thee
(Jeremiah 14:20).

The same Daniel who was put in the lion's den, sat one day meditating on the Word of God. He was reminded that God had promised to return the Israelites to the Promised Land after 70 years of captivity. The 70 years were almost up and they were still in Babylon in bondage. Why? Because the sins and iniquities of their forefathers, the people who had caused them to be exiled, had not been confessed and cleansed. So Daniel, one of the great intercessors of the Old Testament and probably the most godly man of his time, began to fast and pray.

When you read Daniel's prayer in Daniel 9, you may be surprised to discover that this godly man identifies with and confesses the sins and iniquities of his forefathers:

We have sinned, and have committed iniquity, and have
done wickedly, . . . because for our sins, and for the iniquities
of our fathers, Jerusalem and thy people are become a
reproach to all that are about us (Daniel 9:5,16).

When Daniel took the step of confessing the sin and iniquities of his forefathers as if they were his own, God immediately responded. He dispatched the angel Gabriel to Daniel with the answer:

*. . . **while I was still in prayer,** Gabriel, the man I had seen*
in the earlier vision, came to me in swift flight about the
*time of the evening sacrifice. He instructed me . . . **As soon***
***as you began to pray, an answer was given,** which I have*
come to tell you, . . . Seventy 'sevens' are decreed for your
people and your holy city to finish transgression, to put an
end to sin, to atone for wickedness, to bring in everlasting
righteousness, to seal up vision and prophecy and to anoint
the most holy (Daniel 9:21-24 NIV).

This story typifies what many of you may face today: you are born again yet you still remain in bondage to generation sins. Perhaps the missing element in your deliverance is the same as it was for the Israelites in Daniel's day: the acknowledgment and confession of your iniquities and those of your forefathers.

That confession was just what God was waiting for. He began immediately to implement His plan of deliverance for Israel. I believe that God will do exactly the same thing for you as you acknowledge and confess the sins and iniquities of your forefathers. Put your list of family iniquities before the Lord and get the cleansing. The blood of Jesus will cleanse your bloodline and God will release His power to deliver your family tree from generation iniquities.

Forgive Your Forefathers of Family Iniquities

You may not feel very forgiving toward your forefathers because their iniquities have caused you such problems. You must guard against the "victim" attitude, however. You aren't a victim in Christ Jesus; you're a victor. Your forefathers may have passed along to you a weakness for the enemy to use against you, but you make the choice. To break the cycle of iniquity for yourself and the next generation, you must forgive your forefathers:

> *Forgive us our debts, as we have also forgiven our debtors.*
> *For if you forgive men when they sin against you, your*
> *heavenly Father will also forgive you* (Matthew 6:12,14 NIV).

Many people have been terribly hurt by their parents or other family members. Perhaps you are one of those people and feel you have "a right" to never speak to them again. However, if you don't forgive them you will judge them and your judging will return to haunt you. Romans 2:1 says that whatever you judge others for, you are guilty of doing yourself. Your judging can set up a new family iniquity for you and your children:

> *Therefore thou art inexcusable, O man, whosoever thou art that judgest: for wherein thou judgest another, thou condemnest thyself;* **for thou that judgest doest the same things.**

Ask God To Forgive Specific Sins of Living Forefathers

Forgiving others so that you will be forgiven is very important. You cannot get total freedom from your family iniquities or any painful situation inflicted on you by another until you release them from their transgressions. Forgiving is not denying the sin or trespasses against you, nor denying that you suffered pain because of their actions; nor does forgiving deny the personal cost of another's actions. Choosing to walk in or live a lifestyle of forgiveness is not a sloppy emotional thing; it is very calculated. After counting the cost of others' sins against you—the unpaid debt that transgression has created in your life—you make the decision to cancel their debt when you forgive them. That is how God forgives you, He doesn't ignore your sins, or cover them up. Rather, He looks to the blood of Jesus and stamps your debt, "paid in full." By His grace and with His help you can do the same:

> *Then said Jesus, Father forgive them; for they know not what they do. . . .* (Luke 23:34).

> *And he* [Stephen] *kneeled down, and cried with a loud voice, Lord, lay not this sin to their charge. And when he had said this, he fell asleep* (Acts 7:60).

Confess Your Participation in the Iniquities of Your Forefathers

Don't brush lightly over this step in the process to gain your freedom from family iniquities. We have a tendency to avoid taking blame. There used to be a comedian who excused every mistake he made with the phrase, "The devil made me do it." In light of your new understanding of family iniquities, you must be careful and not excuse your own sins by thinking, "My forefathers made me do that." Your forefathers provided you the spiritual weakness and the devil has no doubt taken advantage of your vulnerability, but never for a moment forget that you—by your free will—commit the sin. You are accountable.

Remember, God will not cover up your trash, overlook your sin, or excuse it because it is a family weakness. God expects you to repent. The consequences for not dealing with sin as a Christian are grave. Unconfessed sin is the mountain made from a mole hill, because by not dealing with sin you give *place* to the devil in your life—you give him a stronghold, a high place, a place of authority from which to operate:

> *He that covereth his sins shall not prosper: but whoso*

confesseth and forsaketh them shall have mercy (Proverbs 28:13).

Neither give place to the devil (Ephesians 4:27).

The consequences of not confessing your sins are terrible, but the rewards for taking responsibility and facing God with them are wonderful. God will give you mercy, forgiveness, and cleansing from "all" unrighteousness. The God of love loved you before you were born again and loves you just as much now. It doesn't matter how grievous your sin or how badly you feel you have blown it and disappointed Him. God is like the father of the prodigal son, waiting with open arms to hug you, clasp you to Himself, and return you to your rightful place in His kingdom. Like the prodigal son, you may be dirty and smelly from wallowing with the pigs, but God doesn't care about your hygiene; He'll clean you up. He wants you to come home:

. . . But where sin abounded, grace did much more abound (Romans 5:20).

Ask God To Forgive and Cleanse You

Now that you have confessed—accepted the responsibility for—your sin, ask God to forgive and cleanse you and He will:

*But if we walk in the light, as he is in the light, we have fellowship one with another, **and the blood of Jesus Christ his Son cleanseth us from all sin.** If we say that we have no sin, we deceive ourselves, and the truth is not in us. If we confess our sins, he is faithful and just to forgive us our sins, and to cleanse us from all unrighteousness* (I John 1:7-9).

Now pray this prayer with me:

Father, I thank You for Your Word which is a lamp unto my feet and a light unto my path. I thank You for redemption through the blood of Jesus. I give myself to You. I ask You to cleanse me from all sin and iniquity. Forgive us—myself, my parents, and my forefathers—of all unrighteousness. Cleanse me now by the blood from all sins, diseases,

*infirmities, and attitudes that are not like You. I believe that
You are breaking the link of iniquity and delivering me, my
children, and the next generation from the bondage of
hereditary weaknesses. In Jesus' name. Amen!*

Submit Your Will to God

Each step we have covered is important, but this next step is what
will lock-in your freedom from bondage, and permanently put family
iniquities in your past. The key is to "submit." Adam's sin was one of
rebellion against God and the opposite of rebellion is submission. Jesus
submitted to the Father and so must we. Submission is not being God's
robot but rather choosing to accept God's plan for your life. It is saying:
"You are the Creator and I'm the created. I accept Your Lordship over
me. Your plan is better than my plan and I want to do things Your
way." God is, this moment, at work in the area of your will because
it is vital to the completion of your victory:

> *. . . continue to work out your salvation with fear and
> trembling, for it is **God who works in you to will and to
> act according to his good purpose** (Philippians 2:12,13 NIV).*

God cannot supernaturally empower your unsubmitted will. Until
your will is in agreement with His will, you are operating under your
own power. It isn't God's purpose to break your will, He wants you
to end your rebellion so you can find your victory. God's order for your
victory is "submit" to Him and "resist" the devil. Once you have
submitted, you are enabled to *successfully* resist the devil:

> *. . . Submit yourselves, then, to God. **Resist the devil, and
> he will flee from you** (James 4:7 NIV).*

Jesus Suffered the Curse and Overcame the Devil for You

Have you suffered enough yet? Some people feel they must suffer
the guilt and shame of their sins themselves. Stop it! You insult the
work of Christ on the Cross by continuing to live in guilt and shame
for your past sins and iniquities:

Christ hath redeemed us from the curse of the law, being

made a curse for us: for it is written, Cursed is every one
that hangeth on a tree: That the blessing of Abraham might
come on the Gentiles, through Jesus Christ; that we might
receive the promise of the Spirit through faith
(Galatians 3:13,14).

Who gave himself for us, that he might **redeem us from**
all iniquity, and purify unto himself a peculiar people,
zealous of good works (Titus 2:14).

You are the "righteousness of God" through the blood of Jesus. God sees you not as *guilty* but as *righteous*. God is not ashamed of you, He is proud of you. You did not earn this position with God by any good deeds or by acts of penitence. It's part of the package of salvation. It is time to bring your self-image in line with God's view of you:

For he had made him to be sin for us, who knew no sin;
that we might be made the righteousness of God in him
(II Corinthians 5:21).

God's Word says that you are healed not only of your diseases but of the shame and guilt of your sins, iniquities, and trespasses. Receive by faith *a healing* in your thinking:

But he was wounded for our transgressions, he was bruised
for our iniquities: the chastisement of our peace was upon
him; **and with his stripes we are healed** (Isaiah 53:5).

Perhaps you recall from an earlier chapter Satan's victory when Adam sinned. Satan believed that he had won. Man was a casualty of the conflict but the devil didn't care. God, however, cares about you! God loves people! He sent Jesus to take the punishment for your sin and reverse the curse of your family iniquities:

. . . For this purpose the Son of God was manifested, that
he might destroy the works of the devil [in your life]
(I John 3:8).

God Has All Authority

You need to understand your line of authority. Do you have authority? What is it? How does it work? Why should God give it to you?

God is the source for all authority and power. He is King of kings

70

and Lord of lords. A proud King Nebuchadnezzar learned this lesson the hard way but finally looked up to heaven and said:

> . . . *he* [God] *doeth according to his will in the army of heaven, and among the inhabitants of the earth: and none can stay his hand, or say unto him, What doest thou?* (Daniel 4:35).

God delegated His authority to Jesus. Let's pull back the curtain and watch the passing of the scepter of power through the eyes of Daniel:

> *In my vision at night I looked, and there before me was one like a son of man* [Jesus], *coming with the clouds of heaven. He approached the Ancient of Days* [God] *and was led into his presence. He was given authority, glory and sovereign power; all peoples, nations and men of every language worshiped him. His dominion is an everlasting dominion that will not pass away, and his kingdom is one that will never be destroyed* (Daniel 7:13 NIV).

Jesus delegated His authority to believers. You can't earn it. You don't deserve it in your own right; nevertheless, Jesus *gave* you the gift of authority. Take the scepter of His authority and use it to be set free from your family iniquities:

> *I have given you* **authority** *to trample on snakes and scorpions and* **to overcome all the power of the enemy; nothing will harm you** (Luke 10:19 NIV).

Use the Authority of the Name of Jesus

Don't allow the commonality of the name of Jesus to cause you to forget the raw power of that name. "Jesus" is the name above every name. Devils quiver at that name, angels launch into flight at that name, the sick are healed by the power of the name—Jesus. No evil thing can stand against the name of Jesus. At the name of Jesus your family iniquities have no choice but to bow:

> . . . **In my name** *they will drive out demons; they will speak in new tongues; they will pick up snakes with their hands; and when they drink deadly poison, it will not hurt them at all; they will place their hands on sick people, and they*

will get well (Mark 16:17,18 NIV).

*. . . I tell you the truth, my Father will give you whatever you ask **in my name.** Until now you have not asked for anything **in my name.** Ask and you will receive, and your joy will be complete* (John 16:23,24 NIV).

Why did Jesus give you power through His name? To bring glory to God. When you get free from your family iniquities—the strongholds and high places of the enemy in your life, in the lives of your children, and the next generation—think of the pleasure that victory brings to God. The devil may have had the first laugh when he seduced Adam and Eve to sin, but God has the last laugh when the hold of sin and Satan is broken off your life:

*And I will do whatever you ask **in my name,** so that the Son may bring glory to the Father. You may ask me for anything **in my name,** and I will do it* (John 14:13,14 NIV).

Declare the Power of the Blood of Jesus

Without the precious blood of Jesus, all the preceding steps of deliverance are as nothing. It is His blood that cleanses you from sin and iniquity; reconciles you to the Father; gives you the victory over death and the grave; and makes "all things possible." The steps to your victory over family iniquities begin and end at the Cross and with the shed blood of Christ. Satan was completely fooled, He thought you were sentenced without parole—no pardon was possible. But God loved you so much He sent Jesus to die for your freedom:

*Jesus replied, I tell you the truth, everyone who sins is a slave to sin. Now a slave has no permanent place in the family, but a son belongs to it forever. **So if the Son sets you free, you will be free indeed*** (John 8:34-36 NIV).

In fact, the law requires that nearly everything be cleansed with blood, and without the shedding of blood there is no forgiveness (Hebrews 9:22 NIV).

Declare Your Curses Are Broken

It is time for you to make a faith declaration concerning your family iniquities. You are full of God's Word, and the Word has built your faith. Declare boldly, using your God-given authority, your total victory over every family iniquity. Name each and every thing that has caused you to be less than a victor. Call both heaven and hell to witness your emancipation proclamation. Your faith-filled testimony is the final straw to break the devil's back:

> *And they overcame him by the blood of the Lamb, and by the **word of their testimony;** and they loved not their lives unto the death* (Revelation 12:11).

Your faith-filled words are the match that ignites the dynamite that will explode the family iniquities from your life. God's power and authority in you is like a coiled spring waiting for release. It is only *potential power* until you release it with words into your area of need:

> *. . . Have faith in God. For verily I say unto you, That **whosoever shall say** unto this mountain, Be thou removed, and be thou cast into the sea; and shall not doubt in his heart, but shall believe that **those things which he saith shall come to pass; he shall have whatsoever he saith**￼* (Mark 11:22,23).

Your words have authority both in heaven and on earth. Your mouth has the power to "bind" the works of Satan—family iniquities—and to "loose" the blessings of God in your life:

> *. . . Whatsoever ye shall bind on earth shall be bound in heaven . . .* (Matthew 18:18).

What you speak to yourself about yourself, is also vitally important. Did you know that you have already died and been buried? It's true. When you received salvation you were *identified* with Jesus' death and resurrection. Begin saying to yourself, "I am dead to sin and alive unto God":

> *Knowing this, that our old man is crucified with him, that the body of sin might be destroyed, that henceforth we should not serve sin* (Romans 6:6).

> *Likewise reckon ye also yourselves to be dead indeed unto*

sin, but alive unto God through Jesus Christ our lord (Romans 6:11).

Speak Blessings Over Your Life and the Lives of Your Children

What you say about yourself and your family is more important than what others say about you. Your words have power. You can bless or curse yourself and your family by what you say. By speaking the blessings from God's Word, you release God's best into your situations. You have a heritage of blessing from your heavenly Father, speak it over yourself and your children:

Christ hath redeemed us from the curse . . . That the blessing of Abraham might come on the Gentiles through Jesus Christ . . . (Galatians 3:13,14).

Praise be to the God and Father of our Lord Jesus Christ, who has blessed us in the heavenly realms with every spiritual blessing in Christ (Ephesians 1:3 NIV).

Now live as though the curse of your family iniquities is defeated and has been replaced with the blessings of God, because it's true. Your fresh start, your new day has come!

Worksheet

The following are the steps included in this chapter to help you break the pattern of generation iniquities in your life, once and for all. Write down your response to each step so that you may refer to it from time to time. Don't rush; take as long as each step requires.

First step: Allow the Holy Spirit to bring to your remembrance the sins and iniquities of your parents and forefathers and confess them. (See page 63.)

☑

☐ Write the name of each of your forefathers as far back as you can remember. (If you don't know their names, write their relationship to you, i.e., great-grandfather, great-grandmother.)

_____

_____

_____

_____

_____

☐ As you meditate on each person, write down the iniquities they were involved in. Take the time necessary to be as thorough as possible.

_____

_____

_____

_____

_____

☐ Confess, as if they were your own, your forefathers' iniquities.

Second Step: Personally forgive your forefathers of their iniquities. (See page 66.)

☐ Look at your list and starting with the most distant of your deceased forefathers, ask God to forgive each of their iniquities.

Third Step: Ask God to forgive specific sins of your living forefathers.

(See page 66.)

☐ Review the iniquities of your living parents and grandparents.

☐ Make a faith decision to forgive—to cancel their debt—those who have wounded you by their sins and iniquities.

Fourth Step: Confess your participation in the iniquities of your family tree. (See page 67.)

☐ Accept the responsibility for your own iniquities.

☐ Avoid creating a stronghold for the devil by confessing your participation in your forefathers' iniquities to God.

Fifth Step: Ask God to forgive and cleanse you. (See page 68.)

☐ Having accepted responsibility and confessed your participation in family iniquities, ask forgiveness.

Sixth Step: Submit your will to God. (See page 69.)

☐ Submit to God's plan for your life to lock-in your victory.

☐ Your submitted "will" is supernaturally empowered to make you an overcomer.

Seventh Step: Jesus suffered the curse and overcame the devil for you. (See page 69.)

☐ Jesus bore your shame. You don't have to carry it.

☐ Allow God to heal and transform a sin consciousness into righteousness consciousness.

Eighth Step: God has all authority. (See page 70.)

☐ God has all authority and has delegated it to Jesus.

☐ Jesus has delegated His authority to every born again believer, and has empowered you to be free of family iniquities and all the works of the devil.

Ninth Step: Use the authority of the name of Jesus. (See page 71.)

☐ Apply the name "Jesus" to your family iniquities; at the name of Jesus, everything that is named must come under His authority and the authority of the believer who uses His name. (See Philippians 2:10.)

Tenth Step: Declare the power of the blood of Jesus. (See page 72.)

☐ Jesus purchased your freedom from every family iniquity by his shed blood.

Eleventh Step: Declare your family's generation curses are broken. (See page 73.)

☐ Using your list of family iniquities, name each iniquity and speak faith-filled words to proclaim your victory over each one.

☐ Release the power of God into each situation by your words— the blood of Jesus and your testimony will overcome the devil. (See Revelation 12:11.)

☐ Use your authority to bind the work of the enemy and loose the blessings of God into your life and the lives of your children.

☐ Speak only God's truth about your family iniquities; you are dead to sin and alive to God.

Twelfth Step: Speak blessings over your life and the lives of your children. (See page 74.)

☐ Be careful to speak ONLY blessings (what the Bible says about you) over yourself and your family, because your words have the power to bless or to curse.

Chapter Seven
FREE INDEED!

If the Son therefore shall make you free, ye shall be free indeed (John 8:36).

In the previous chapter, *"Breaking the Pattern . . . Once and For All,"* we covered the various steps necessary for breaking the generation curse and establishing a heritage of blessings.

When you were born again, your family iniquities were not just broken; they were reversed and God blessed you in the areas that used to be cursed. Now, you are free indeed! Not that you'll never have to contend with the iniquities of the past again, but you have taken an important step in reversing your family's curse. In the area that you were weak, you are now strong. You have set the course for your family's future, and you can begin by faith to walk in generation blessings.

Abundant Life

The Word of God promises you an abundant life. The iniquities that you and your family have labored under for so many years did not actually belong to you. Exodus 20:5 says that the sins of the forefathers are passed down to the third and fourth generations of those who hate God. If you are born again, you can rest assured that the love of God has been poured out in your heart by the Holy Spirit and you don't meet the qualifications for a generation curse. (See Romans 5:5.) Those who love Him, He blesses unto a thousand generations.

You might ask, "Well, if I'm born again and Jesus has blessed the areas of my life that used to be cursed, why didn't those iniquities cease to operate in my life?" Because the areas were never dealt with. For the most part, Christians come against the symptoms and not the root cause of a thing. For example, if your child misbehaves in school, you would probably focus on the misbehaving instead of searching out the root cause, which could be a classroom bully or a verbally abusive teacher. Unless you know what the Bible says about you and your inheritance in Christ, the devil will continue to bully you *even after salvation,* killing, stealing from, and destroying you and the future members of your family tree.

Sanctification of the Soul

At the time of your born-again experience, there was no question that you received a new spirit and a new nature. You received the incorruptible Seed, Jesus Christ, Who sanctified you and set you apart for the Master's use. The real you, your recreated spirit, no longer wanted to sin against God. Although the inward man may have desired to refrain from past sins, I'm sure that many of you will admit to still blowing it from time to time because of the mystery of iniquity still at work in your old nature. Why? Because *parts* of you were surrendered to the Lordship of Jesus Christ, and not your entire being.

The word, *sanctification*, means "to make holy, consecrate, to set apart." Many in the Body of Christ are aware of the sanctifying work that takes place in their spirits at the time of salvation, but few seem to understand that this process must also take place in their souls, where the mind, will, and emotions reside:

> And may the God of peace Himself sanctify you through
> and through—that is, separate you from profane things,
> make you pure and wholly consecrated to God—and may
> your spirit and soul and body be preserved sound and
> complete [and found] blameless at the coming of our Lord
> Jesus Christ, . . . (I Thessalonians 5:23 TAB).

Until your soul is sanctified or set apart and holy unto the Lord, a door is left open for the bruises of family iniquities to continue to reign in you and your future generations. We've all heard horror stories about upstanding Christian men and women who led exemplary lives but were closet alcoholics or molested their children.

Sin begins in the soul, therefore, sanctification must take place there also. A person who is caught stealing didn't just wake up one day and decide to become a thief. No, he entertained the idea in his mind long before he decided to act upon it.

One of the best ways I have found to sanctify your soul is through reading the Word of God, which washes your mind, will, and emotions of everything that could hinder the will of God. Although this topic is dealt with more thoroughly in chapter 8, daily Bible reading can cleanse your soul of the evil seeds that could defile it. You may think it is all right for you to become angry, hold bitterness in your heart, or nurse a grudge; however, I Thessalonians 5:23 says your "whole" spirit, soul, and body must be sanctified. The writer of James bears witness to this truth:

> From whence come wars and fightings among you? come they not hence, even of your lusts that war in your members? (James 4:1).

Sanctification of the soul is a process. Consequently, you may have surrendered parts of your being (your spirit and perhaps your body) to the Lordship of Jesus Christ, but the *whole* man must be sanctified or set apart for the Master's use. One of the purposes of breaking the pattern of generation iniquities in chapter 6 is to allow this sanctifying process to take place so that you will have complete and total freedom in Christ in every area of your life.

The Blessings of Abraham

> And I will bless them that bless thee; and curse him that curseth thee: . . . (Genesis 12:3).

Your family blessings are guaranteed. Abraham received the blessings of God by faith. When Balaam was summoned to curse the Israelites, he could not because they had been blessed in Abraham's loins. The king of Moab became angry with Balaam and said, "Why don't you curse these people? I've told you to curse them, and you keep blessing them!" Balaam answered, "You just can't curse what God has blessed" (see Numbers 23:8).

The same principle holds true for you and your family tree. You have come into the knowledge of the truth of God's Word about generation blessings, and you will never be satisfied by accepting anything less than His best. You now know that you will never again have to put up with the devil's junk. If symptoms resurface of something that has been reversed, you can stand your ground and speak God's Word to that area of your life. You can tell the devil that Galatians 3:13 says you've been redeemed from the curse, and only blessings can be inherited by your family tree.

One mistake many Christians make is thinking they can defeat the devil once and for all. No, the devil may come at you with the same generation weaknesses time and time again. Just remind him that it is written . . .

The Wounds of a Trespass

A sanctified soul is one that is healed and whole in Christ Jesus, and the wounds of a trespass cannot enter. The mind, will, and emotions have been cleansed of past hurts and iniquities, and they are free to submit to the Lordship of Jesus Christ.

Wounds from a trespass adversely impact the mind, will, and emotions, and cut right to the core of a person. Unlike a natural wound that scabs over and eventually heals, soulish wounds can only be healed by the blood of Jesus. Otherwise, they will fester and spread like cancer.

Wounds to the soul are caused by trespasses. If you'll recall from chapter 1, to *trespass* means to "overstep preestablished boundaries." For the purposes of this chapter, to trespass also implies the violation of another person's being.

There are many types of trespasses. You can trespass against someone verbally by the words you speak to or about them, or by committing acts of violence or incest against them. Everyone has experienced the wound of a trespass, and either intentionally or unintentionally, we have all trespassed against others.

To *trespass* also means to wound or "mar." When you trespass against someone and wound them (or vice versa), you literally mar them or leave a mark or bruise on them that hurts so badly and penetrates so deeply, they'll remember it for the rest of their lives.

Proverbs 18:8 says, *"The words of a talebearer are as wounds, and they go down into the innermost parts of the belly."* From this scripture we can deduce that the old saying, "Sticks and stones may break my bones, but words will never hurt me" is just another lie of the devil. A trespass is a very lethal thing.

In II Corinthians 12:7, the apostle Paul talks about a thorn in the flesh that was a messenger of Satan sent to buffet him. You can well believe that the trespasses that have been committed against you are thorns or messengers of Satan, sent to vex you and thwart the will

82

of God for your life and your future generations.

If you are carrying wounds from trespasses committed against you or that you have committed against others, this is your opportunity to release the guilt and pain and to go free! Although Jesus set you free from sin at the time of the new birth, many Christians will continue to hold onto the wounds caused by trespasses so they can nurse them. They'll suppress the hurt until something happens that triggers the memory of the pain. Then they'll relive the experience all over again. Although some people find comfort in this, holding onto these trespasses is the root of bitterness, which the writer of Hebrews says will spring up and defile you (see Hebrews 12:15). The blood of Jesus is powerful enough to cleanse you from sins and trespasses.

Family Trespasses

Trespasses hurt people and can also destroy family relations. They are very serious offenses to God. Like sin, transgression, and iniquity, trespassing began in the Garden of Eden with Adam and Eve. After they transgressed against God by eating of the fruit of the tree, the "mystery of iniquity" was set in motion and passed down to their future generations. In Genesis 4, their son, Cain, began a family iniquity when he murdered his brother Abel. This was a trespass, and Abel's blood cried out from the earth for vengeance.

In Genesis 31:36, Jacob was angry with his uncle, Laban, and demanded to know: "What is my trespass?" Jacob knew firsthand what a trespass was because he had trespassed against his brother, Esau, on many occassisons. He met his match, however, when he met Laban, who trespassed against Jacob at every available opportunity. Not only did Laban exact seven years labor from Jacob and then give him the wrong wife, he also made him work another seven years for the wife he'd initially promised, and changed Jacob's wages 10 times.

After the wrestling match with the angel and his subsequent name change, Jacob, now called Israel, commanded his son Joseph to forgive his brothers for the trespasses they had committed against him. If you'll recall, Joseph's brothers despised him because their father favored him, and because they recognized the call of God on his life. They stole the many-colored coat his father had made just for him, threw Joseph into a pit, threatened to kill him, sold him as a slave to the Midianites, and lied to their father about what had happened to him.

Although a trespass can deeply hurt you, and his brothers' actions could have severely wounded Joseph, he chose to forgive them. He understood that what had happened to him was a part of God's plan to make, mold, and exalt him; and to preserve the posterity of the Israelites.

No matter how great the trespass, you can still be set free of the wound it has caused because of the provision Jesus made at Calvary. Joseph was overcome emotionally and wept on several occassions when God reunited him to his family. He also wept when his brothers asked for forgiveness. I believe he wept most when the thorn or mark of what his brothers had done was heavily upon him. His weeping was God's way of releasing him from the effects of their trespasses against him, and setting him free to forgive and to be free indeed!

True Confessions

According to Leviticus 5, when an Israelite trespassed against someone, they had to bring a sin offering *and* a fifth of what the offering would cost as an atonement for their sin. If their offering was a lamb, for example, then they had to also bring 20 percent of what the lamb would cost and give it to the priest as their trespass offering. I believe the trespass offering was set up this way because when you are held accountable for your actions and it costs you something, you are more likely to remember the consequences of your behavior if you are ever tempted to do it again.

Jesus is our High Priest, and we can take our trespass offerings directly to Him. Once a trespass becomes a pattern of sin, however, it becomes an iniquity that is passed from generation to generation. If you'll recall from previous chapters, iniquities can only be broken by confessing them, repenting for your forefathers' participation and the part you have played in perpetuating them, and applying the blood of Jesus.

There is a group of people in the United States who are visiting places where the American Indians were used and abused, and repenting to them and asking for forgiveness for the trespasses that both they and their forefathers' committed against them. I also know of people who are going into parts of Africa and praying over places where Africans were sold into slavery. Why? Because when you repent of your trespasses, you bring a cleansing into the situation:

> If they shall confess their iniquity, and the iniquity of their fathers, with their trespass which they trespassed against me, and that also they have walked contrary unto me; And that I also have walked contrary unto them, and have brought them into the land of their enemies; if then their uncircumcised hearts be humbled, and they then accept of the punishment of their iniquity, Then will I remember my covenant with Jacob ... and I will remember the land (Leviticus 26:40-42).

Standing in the Gap

During the period in which David was fleeing from Saul, it was his custom to protect the sheep of a man named Nabal from the thieves and robbers who would attempt to steal them. It was sheep shearing time and Nabal was hosting a huge celebration and David and his men were hungry.

David sent 10 of his men to Nabal and asked, "Could you possibly share some of your sheep with us? My men and I have a need, and after all, we've helped protect both your men and your sheep." Nabal, being the arrogant and haughty person that he was, responded with:

> ... Who is David? ... Shall I then take my bread, and my water, and my flesh that I have killed for my shearers, and give it unto men, whom I know not whence they be?
> (I Samuel 25:10,11).

When David's men told him of Nabal's response, David prepared for war. However, when Abigail, Nabal's wife, heard what had happened, she immediately went to meet David and his band and to intercede on behalf of her husband:

*Then Abigail made haste, and took two hundred loaves, and
two bottles of wine, and five sheep ready dressed, and five
measures of parched corn, and an hundred clusters of
raisins, and two hundred cakes of figs, and laid them on
asses* (I Samuel 25:18).

When she saw David and his 400 men, she jumped off her donkey
and begged him to forgive Nabal of his trespass against him. She said:

*. . . Upon me, my lord, upon me let this iniquity be . . . forgive
the trespass of thine handmaid: for the LORD will certainly
make my lord a sure house; because my lord fighteth the
battles of the LORD, and evil hath not been found in thee
all thy days* (I Samuel 25:24,28).

Abigail said, "Let my husband's trespass come on me." I'm sure many
people would say, "I have enough problems of my own to contend with,
I don't need to take responsibility for my spouse's as well. He's big
enough to take up for himself. I'll just be a rich widow. I'll buy a yacht
and sail around the world." Instead, Abigail stood in the gap for her
husband, confessed his sin and trespass as though they were her own,
and brought a cleansing into the situation by bridging the gap between
David and Nabal.

Ezekiel 22:30 says, *"And I sought for a man among them, that should
make up the hedge, and stand in the gap before me for the land, that
I should not destroy it: but I found none."* If you want to see yourself
and someone else released from a trespass, then become a gap stander.
Because Abigail stood in the gap for Nabal, it softened David's heart
and he didn't kill them. If you'll remember, God brought judgment
on Nabal and he died, and David married Abigail and she became
a queen.

The human nature is to be a gap finder instead of a gap stander.
People are so willing to point out the gaps of others instead of praying
to God to forgive them for their behavior. This is what Stephen did
in Acts 7:60 when he was being stoned. He could have called fire down
from heaven, but he chose to look heavenward and said, *". . . Lord,
lay not this sin to their charge. And when he said this, he fell asleep."*

Jesus' Provision

Make a quality decision right now to forgive everyone who has ever trespassed against you according to Matthew 18:35 and Luke 17:4. Ask God to forgive them as well. Isaiah 53 says Jesus was wounded for your trespasses. You may be reading this book and you're as wounded as you can be. You keep going over and over your wounds, licking them like a child does when he's pulled the scab off a wound and it begins to bleed. You lick your wounds and you tell everybody about them.

I know a woman who is owed some money by someone who has failed to repay her. Everyday she goes over this trepass. "This person owes me money, this person owes me money." Every week she calls or writes this person to say, "You owe me X-amount of money." She licks and licks this wound and keeps it real moist. Until she forgives this person of the debt owed to her, her wound will never heal.

Matthew 18:15 tells you that people are going to trespass against you and what to do when this happens. Instead of doing what most people do when someone trespasses against them, you are instructed to "*. . . go and tell him his fault between thee and him alone: . . . .*" I can tell you that 99 percent of Christians do not go alone and tell a brother his fault. They tell everyone else, first. But God says that if somebody trespasses against you, you should confront them, not in anger, but in a spirit of reconcilliation: "I don't really believe you meant to do this. But this is how it made me feel."

I don't know about you, but I don't like to confront people, and I don't like for them to confront me. I do want to be a doer of the Word, however, so I practice doing what it says. This is the only way to bring healing into a potentially lethal situation. If you don't approach your brother and attempt to clear things up, it could permanently wound or mar him.

Sowing and Reaping

If you had a thorn in your foot and couldn't find it, you would have to depend on someone with a magnifying glass and a pair of tweezers to locate and remove it. Galatians 6:7 says you reap what you sow.

If you sow forgiveness, you will reap it. And as you forgive, the Word will set you free and give life to those areas that have been dead because of trespasses and overcome with weeds and thorns. The magnifying glass of the Holy Spirit will locate each thorn in your heart and pull it out. He'll purge you with the blood of Jesus, and apply the balm of Gilead to those areas and make you whole.

The blood of Jesus has cleansed you and your family tree. You have broken the pattern of generation sins, and your soul has been sanctified by the washing of the water by the Word. You are healed of the trespasses committed against you and the ones you have committed against others. There is no earthly reason for you to remain bound.

You have broken those sinful patterns of your past by the name of Jesus and the blood of the Lamb, turning family iniquities into generation blessings that will continue to the thousandth generation! Blessings, not curses, are your birthright. Truly, whom the Son has set free is free indeed, and this promise is for you and the next generation!

SECTION THREE

THE NEXT GENERATION

Chapter Eight

BEGINNING YOUR
HERITAGE OF BLESSINGS

Throughout the pages of this book, we have examined some hard-hitting elements of generation curses and blessings and how they relate to individuals and their family trees. In Section 1, we examined the origin of the generation curse. In Section 2, we saw that through His death, burial, and resurrection, Jesus reversed the curse and *all* born-again believers were set free to inherit generation blessings.

In this chapter we will examine some very specific things you can do to begin your heritage of blessings. Yes, Y-O-U can directly impact the spiritual growth of your family and cause it to grow in good soil with a strong, healthy root system that will produce life and not death. If you have already followed the steps to cleanse your family tree through personal and/or national repentance, forgiveness, and the shed blood of Jesus, then you have begun a process that will reap eternal benefits.

To use the analogy of a plant that is dying because it is planted in poor or bad soil: once a family tree is cleansed of its iniquities, it too must be repotted from the "bad," unfruitful soil of the past, to the new, fertile soil of Jesus Christ. Once you've completed this process, you can begin to focus on establishing blessings for this and the next generation, and maintaining these blessings and nurturing a mature family tree.

The Good Soil

In nature, to grow a healthy, mature tree, the tree must be planted in good, fertile soil. The same is true for your family tree. To begin a heritage of blessings, you must plant the seed of God's Word in your own heart as well as in the hearts of your family members. The spiritual seed that you plant must be planted in "good" ground, which in God's kingdom is symbolized by the heart. It is in the heart that the Word of God is planted, and it is in the heart that the Word of God bears much, little, or no fruit. Jesus likened the heart to the "types" of soil that the Word is planted in:

A farmer went out to sow his seed. As he was scattering the seed, some fell along the path [the way side]; *it was trampled on, and the birds of the air ate it up. Some fell on rock [rocky ground], and when it came up, the plants withered because they had no moisture. Other seed fell among thorns, which grew up with it and choked the plants. Still other seed fell on good soil. It came up and yielded a crop, a hundred times more than was sown...* (Luke 8:5-8 NIV).

This is the meaning of the parable: The seed is the word of God. Those along the path are the ones who hear, and then the devil comes and takes away the word from their hearts, so that they may not believe and be saved. Those on the rock are the ones who receive the word with joy when they hear it, but they have no root. They believe for a while, but in the time of testing they fall away. The seed that fell among thorns stands for those who hear, but as they go on their way they are choked by life's worries, riches and pleasures, and they do not mature. But the seed on good soil stands for those with a notable and good heart, who hear the word, retain it, and by persevering produce a crop (Luke 8:11-15 NIV).

The "path" or "way side" is the first type of soil Jesus mentions. It represents a person whose understanding of the Word is in his head only and not his heart. He mentally assents that the Word of God is true, but lacks spiritual depth and understanding. Consequently the devil has little or no difficulty stealing the Word that was sown in this person's heart.

The rocky ground is symbolic of the person who joyfully receives the Word as truth but has a superficial understanding of it. When the pressures of life and temptations come to challenge his level of commitment to be a doer of the Word he has received, he becomes fainthearted and walks away. The seed that is sown in this type of ground soon withers and dies.

The heart with the thorny ground is the third type of soil. Like the Word sown in the rocky ground, the person whose heart is thorny will also receive the Word as truth. However, the cares, riches, and pleasures of this world choke the Word and cause it to become unfruitful.

Seed sown into the "good" ground, according to this scripture, yields a crop 100 times more than what was sown. This person's heart is ripe for the Word—it is pure and holy before the Father. The King James version of Luke 8:15 says that the heart of this person is honest and good; having heard the Word, he keeps or does it, and bears fruit with patience.

I once heard a well-known speaker say, "A good marriage takes work, and a bad marriage takes even more work." This same principle is true when it comes to establishing a godly family tree. Even when the seed is sown in good soil, there are things that must be done to cultivate a good crop or harvest.

As is true in nature, the soil must be cultivated before the seed you sow will reap a bountiful harvest. If you sow seed on hard, barren ground, you can expect to receive little, if any, results. As a matter of fact, one of the purposes of praise and worship in our church services is to usher in God's presence and to prepare the congregation's hearts to receive the Word of God. Although the Word can be delivered without this cultivating process, you will find that the congregation is less receptive because they are still consumed with thoughts and the events of the day as opposed to focusing on the things of God.

Cultivating your family tree is a very simple process. All you have to do is make a quality decision and commitment to apply the Word of God to *every area* of your life. In doing this, you are uprooting any weeds of iniquity that might be present, and tilling your heart and your family's to receive the Word. As it does in nature, the seed of the Word undergoes a process; you must allow time for it to germinate, sprout, and grow before it produces the desired fruit. The more skillful you become at cultivating your heart and your family's, the more fertile your hearts will become and the more fruit you will produce as you receive the good seed—God's Word.

Feeding the Tree

As newborn babes, desire the sincere milk of the word, that ye may grow thereby (I Peter 2:2).

*Whom shall he teach knowledge? and whom shall he make
to understand doctrine? them that are weaned from the milk,
and drawn from the breasts* (Isaiah 28:9).

Feeding your family tree is a process that takes place over a period
of time, and not just a one-time thing. After you have sown the seed
for a good family tree, you must care for and nurture it. To *nurture*
means "to feed and protect; to nurture one's offspring; to support and
encourage as during the period of training or development; to bring
up; train."

One of the basic ways you nurture your tree is to feed it (your family)
the Word of God. This can be done through regular family devotions
and/or Scripture memorization. You will also need to block out a certain
portion of your day in which you "discuss" the Word with your family.
Perhaps the best time for your family to do this is the first thing in
the morning or before or after dinner. The choice is up to you. But,
there needs to be an emphasis on the Word in your home, in addition
to what your family learns at church.

You're probably thinking, "Marilyn, this is so simple! It's elementary."
That's true, but I've discovered that some of the most profound
revelations I've ever received have been simple. The Word is what will
cause your family to overcome its inherited family iniquities: *"And they
overcame him by the blood of the Lamb, and by **the word** of their
testimony; . . . "* (Revelation 12:11). If you are going to feed your family
spiritually, then you need to start with the Word of God.

Watering the Tree

In order for a tree to grow, it must be watered on a consistent basis.
"How," you might ask, "do you water a family tree?" With the "washing
of the water by the Word"—the sanctifying work of the Holy Spirit—
Who is symbolized in the Scriptures as rivers of living water:

*. . . Jesus stood and cried, saying, If any man thirst, let him
come unto me, and drink. He that believeth on me, as the
scripture hath said, out of his belly shall flow **rivers of living
water*** (John 7:37,38).

Rivers of living water in John 7 refer to the Holy Spirit, Who resides in every born-again believer (see I Corinthians 3:16; 6:19). Because He dwells in you, you have access to the very throne room of God:

But the Counselor, the Holy Spirit, whom the Father will send in my name, will teach you all things and will remind you of everything I have said [the Word you plant in your heart] *to you* (John 14:26 NIV).

But when he, the Spirit of truth, comes, he will guide you into all truth. He will not speak on his own; he will **speak only what he hears,** *and he will* **tell you** *what is yet to come. He will bring glory to me by taking from what is mine and making it known to you. All that belongs to the Father is mine. That is why I said the Spirit will take from what is mine and make it known to you* (John 16:13-15 NIV).

One of the many roles or functions of the Holy Spirit according to John 7:26, is to "*. . . teach you all things, and bring all things to your remembrance, ...*" As you and your family study the Word of God, the Holy Spirit will give you an understanding of the truths being presented to you, and will bring back or remind you of that which you have deposited in your hearts so you can apply the Word to your daily lives.

An example of this would be when you come under persecution and you're about to break down and cry, or lash out in revenge. In the nick of time, however, you hear a still, small voice inside of you that says, "*. . . Love your enemies, bless them that curse you, do good to them that hate you, and pray for them which despitefully use you, and persecute you; . . .* " (Matthew 5:44). And you say to yourself, "Oh yeah, I read that scripture last night." You then obey the voice of God and begin to pray and bless your enemies and as a result, you see a supernatural turnaround in the situation that only God could bring.

This is the watering process. The Holy Spirit will water or give life and meaning to the Word as you and your family apply the Word to your daily lives. The fruit that you will bear from being watered by Him will give you insight and revelation into the mysteries of God, and divine direction for your family. As you and your family plant the

Word in your hearts, the Holy Spirit will water the good seed that you are planting and it will overtake and choke out the weeds from the evil seeds planted by your forefathers generations ago.

In conjunction with the Holy Spirit, you and your family also have a role in the watering process. The part you and your family play can be found in James 1:22: *"But be ye doers of the word, and not hearers only, ..."* In other words, as you and your family follow the leading of the Holy Spirit, you will enable Him to water the seeds that will sprout up into a good, healthy, mature family tree.

Pruning

The pruning of a family tree is just as important as feeding and watering it. When a plant or tree is pruned, all of the dead leaves and limbs are cut off. Anger, laziness, sickness, and a bad attitude are just some examples of dead weights that the Holy Spirit will prune from your family tree.

The purpose of this pruning process is to remove everything that would hinder the natural growth process of that tree. John 15:4,16 promise that as you and your family abide in God and His Word abides in you, you will produce "much" fruit and your fruit shall remain:

> *I AM the True Vine and My Father is the Vinedresser. Any branch in Me that does not bear fruit—that stops bearing— He cuts away (trims off, takes away). And He cleanses and repeatedly prunes every branch that continues to bear fruit, to make it bear more and richer and more excellent fruit* (John 15:1,2 TAB).

We know from nature that whenever you plant something, such as a flower garden, both the good and the bad seed—the weeds—come up together. I've spent many a summer afternoon weeding my garden, but thank God for the Holy Spirit Who does the separating and pruning of our spiritual family trees:

> *. . . The kingdom of heaven is like a man who sowed good seed in his field. But while everyone was sleeping, his enemy came and sowed weeds among the wheat, and went away. When the wheat sprouted and formed heads, then the weeds*

also appeared. The owner's servants came to him and said, 'Sir, didn't you sow good seed in your field? Where then did the weeds come from?' 'An enemy did this,' he replied . . . Let both grow together until the harvest. At that time I will tell the harvesters: First collect the weeds and tie them in bundles to be burned; then gather the wheat and bring it into my barn (Matthew 13:24-28,30 NIV).

As you plant the seed of God's Word in the hearts of you and your family and allow the Holy Spirit to water it, bad seed or family iniquities may surface from time to time. Be assured, however, that a time of separation will come, and the iniquities of the past will be consumed by the Word of God, thus enabling your family to inherit and pass on generation blessings.

I was a school teacher when I became Spirit-filled. I was teaching a literature class, and I read two or three books a week. I loved to read, but the Lord told me to quit reading fiction and to use that time to read the Bible instead. I was obedient and began memorizing one book of the Bible a year.

Although I was unaware of it at the time, God was pruning me during this period of my life. My husband and I didn't know we were called into the ministry. We were newlyweds, but God was getting us ready for the time when He would use us in the ministry.

I can look back now and see the pruning times in my life. God said I had some attitudes that I had to get rid of because they would hinder the call of God on my life. I knew I either had to let Him prune me, or my vines would wither and be fruitless.

Nurturing the Tree for Future Generations

David had a very fruitful family tree. He fed, watered, and pruned it. Although he committed adultery and murder, his repentance turned a family iniquity into a generation blessing.

Psalms 32 was written after David's sin with Bath-sheba and his transgression against Uriah the Hittite were revealed. David dealt with three kinds of sin in this psalm: the sin of "missing the mark" when he had Uriah killed; transgression when he and Bath-sheba committed adultery; and iniquity when he attempted to cover his sin and not confess it:

> *Blessed is he whose transgression is forgiven, whose sin is covered. Blessed is the man unto whom the LORD imputeth not iniquity, and in whose spirit there is no guile. When I kept silence, my bones waxed old through my roaring all the day long. For day and night thy hand was heavy upon me: my moisture is turned into the drought of summer. . . . I acknowledged my sin unto thee, and mine iniquity have I not hid. I said, I will confess my transgressions unto the LORD; and thou forgavest the iniquity of my sin* (Psalms 32:1-5).

David, as well as the other Old Testament saints, seemed to have had a better understanding of sin, transgression, and iniquity than the Body of Christ has today. He probably knew that sexual sin was a weakness or iniquity passed from generation to generation in his family tree. As you follow his descendants, you'll see this iniquity in his sons, Amnon, who raped his half sister, Tamar; and Solomon, who had 700 wives and 300 concubines; and Solomon's son, Rehoboam, who also had many wives and concubines.

When David said, "Blessed is the man whose transgression is forgiven," he was admitting his guilt, repenting to God, and asking His forgiveness. His confession was part of the pruning of his family tree. We know from reading the Scriptures that David loved God and His Word and received revelation from the Holy Spirit. Even so, he was subject to a family iniquity of sexual sin that eventually led to murder. Although it would have been very easy, he did not give up on himself or his family. He allowed God to prune him.

If you'll recall from Section 1, chapter 3, sexual sin is symbolized by the frog. In essence, what David was saying was, "God, I don't want any frogs in my family tree. I want to be free from the weaknesses of my flesh. Create in me a clean heart and renew a right spirit within me."

Had David not confessed, a generation curse of iniquity would have continued in his bloodline, and God would have had to destroy his seed. However, because David was a man after God's heart, many of his descendants walked in generation blessings instead of the curse.

Once David allowed the pruning process to take place and was cleansed of sexual sin, God's promise of posterity and blessing was inherited by the next generation:

> *Now the days of David drew nigh that he should die; and he charged Solomon his son, saying, . . . keep the charge of the LORD thy God, to walk in his ways, to keep his statutes, and his commandments, and his judgments, and his testimonies, as it is written in the law of Moses, that thou mayest prosper in all that thou doest, and whithersoever thou turnest thyself: That the LORD **may continue his word which he spake concerning me,** saying, If **thy children** take heed to their way, to walk before me in truth with all their heart and with all their soul, **there shall not fail thee (said he) a man on the throne of Israel*** (I Kings 2:1,3,4).

Although David committed adultery and had a man murdered, his sins were covered. The blood of Jesus was powerful enough to cleanse David (and you) of his sins, transgressions, and iniquities. God saw David as righteous and blessed his family tree. He said the house of David would never end. And it won't. Jesus came from the seed of David, and we are joint heirs with Him.

The Maturation Process

The maturation process of your family tree is guaranteed as long as you continue to feed your family the Word of God, and allow the Holy Spirit to water and prune it. Maturity is a process that should take place in every Christian's life. Once you have planted a good family tree, there are some very practical things you and your family should do to aid in your spiritual growth and the godly inheritance of the next generation. These things include being water baptized, regular church attendance, daily prayer and Bible reading, and being baptized in the Holy Spirit.

Water Baptism

Being water baptized is more than being immersed in a body of cold water. Water baptism is a picture or symbol of the old nature of a person and his family iniquities passing away, and the new nature of Christ being born in him, thus making him an heir to abundant and eternal life. It is symbolic of Jesus' death, burial and resurrection. I was 23 years old when I was water baptized. I had been sprinkled as a baby, but I needed to obey the Scriptures and repent and be baptized:

> *Then they that gladly received his word were baptized: . . .* (Acts 2:41).

Church Attendance

One of the ways you and your family will grow spiritually is through regular church attendance. There is a corporate anointing or strength that comes from fellowshipping on a regular basis with other believers, and the Holy Spirit will also water the seed of the Word that you and your family have sown in your hearts during your personal times of devotion. God's Word commands you to become a part of a local body:

> *Not forsaking the assembling of ourselves together, as the manner of some is; . . .* (Hebrews 10:25).

During the early days of my ministry, I held home Bible studies. A lady attended once who did not believe in healing. She had had an operation to remove part of her hip bone, and had to stand during the entire Bible study because she experienced great pain if she sat for any amount of time.

"Marilyn, you can't tell me healing is in the Bible," she said, "I don't believe it! I heard the scriptures you taught on, but I think that you are taking them out of context. The doctors are for healing and Jesus is for saving, and the two never meet."

I didn't argue with her. I encouraged her to continue to come and study the Word because she really needed to be healed. She also told me that she and her daughter were going blind. She had inherited this condition from her father and grandfather, who were blind, and now her daughter was also being affected.

One of the women in the Bible study invited her to church. Both the lady and her daughter were present at church when the minister stopped, pointed to where they were sitting, and said, "There is a woman in the balcony and you are having problems with your hip. Stand up. God wants to touch your hip and back."

When she stood up, she felt something warm go all over her body. That night while undressing in her bedroom, her daughter exclaimed, "Mother, you look like you have a hip!" And she did. Needless to say, after this experience both the mother and daughter believed in and received healing for their eyes and they are no longer going blind.

Although we know God is Sovereign and He could have performed these miracles independent of any person, place, or thing, it was because of the Word planted in the heart of this woman during my Bible studies, and the corporate anointing at her colleague's church that enabled the Holy Spirit to water the seed planted and to bring about a harvest of healing.

Daily Prayer

Daily prayer is essential to the success of every Christian and Christian family. Prayer is not only a direct line of communication to your heavenly Father, but it is what helps you to "abide in the vine" as you are admonished to do in John 15. Paul exhorts you to ***"Pray without ceasing"*** (I Thessalonians 5:17).

Before she got married, my daughter Sarah met a young man at a secular university she was attending. She said that she liked him and was seeing him on occasion. She also told me he was not saved and it burdened me. You know how we parents are: we're very watchful of our children.

I don't know why I was so troubled about this young man, but I prayed for him. I didn't think it was good for Sarah to be friendly with him, but try and tell that to a 24 year-old! She told me one day, "Well, mother, he's only a friend." The Lord gave me a scripture to give to Sarah from James that says don't make friends with the world.

The next day I said, "The Lord gave me something I want to share with you." I gave her the scripture and explained to her that I didn't believe she was even supposed to be friends with this man. Well, she was not a happy camper with me or God. She sought God in prayer and said, "Why did you tell my mother; why couldn't You tell me?"

God said, "If I told you, you wouldn't have listened, but if I told someone else, it would make you accountable." Needless to say, Sarah quit seeing the young man.

Daily prayer for you and your family can bring you to a place of trust and fellowship with God. It also can keep the lines of communication open so that God can speak to you and your family, and give you the answers to the challenges you will face in life. A daily prayer life can give you the strength to overcome your family's iniquities, and is a must for the maturation process of you and your family tree.

Daily Bible Reading

If you want to break the curse and establish the blessings in your family tree, then daily Bible reading is a must in every Christian's life. It is the Word that the Holy Spirit will water as you and your family mature in the things of God:

> *Study to shew thyself approved unto God, a workman that needeth not to be ashamed, rightly dividing the word of truth* (II Timothy 2:15).

It is very important that Christians feed themselves the Word of God. People will tell me, "I'm just not fed at my church." My response to them is, "Do you have a Bible?" They respond, "Yes." I'll say, "Can you read?" Their answer of course is, "Yes." Then I will ask, "Then why don't you feed yourself?"

Depending on your church to feed you and your family is not enough. You have to feed on the Word daily. As a matter of fact, you and your family should make it a habit of reading through the Bible every year. If you read two Old Testament chapters and one New Testament chapter six days a week, and three Old Testament and two New Testament chapters once a week, you will have read through the Bible in one year! (I publish a Bible-reading plan every month in my ministry magazine, OUTPOURING.) Reading through the Bible on a daily basis will keep you and your family clean of generation iniquities, encouraged about the things of God, and walking in His promises. Nothing can beat it!

Baptism of the Holy Spirit

When you become born again, you are born of the Spirit. However, to enhance the power of your prayers as well as your understanding of the Word, you and your children, and your children's children can be baptized in the Holy Spirit and be filled with the power of God:

> *But ye shall receive power, after that the Holy Ghost is come upon you: . . .* (Acts 1:8).

> *For the promise is unto you, and to your children, and to all that are afar off, even as many as the Lord our God shall call* (Acts 2:39).

The Holy Spirit in your life is your well of living water that Jesus spoke about in John 7:38. He said, He who believes in Me, as the Scripture said, From his innermost being shall flow rivers of living water. The Holy Spirit wants to be a river of living water to your innermost being. He wants to refresh you spiritually:

> *But whosoever drinketh of the water that I shall give him shall never thirst; but the water that I shall give him shall be in him a well of water springing up to everlasting life* (John 4:14).

You are not "less saved" if you aren't baptized in the Holy Spirit; neither are you "more saved" if you are. God wants you to be baptized with the Holy Spirit so that He can empower you spiritually, just as Jesus was empowered spiritually. You were already given the Holy Spirit when you were born again. Now you just have to receive His baptism. By doing so you are receiving His fullness into every area of your life, into every "room" of your being.

It is God's will for you to be born again, water baptized, and filled with the Holy Spirit. It's up to you! The baptism of the Holy Spirit is God's miracle to bring His character and power into your life so that you can be a bold witness for Him:

> *That he would grant you, according to the riches of his glory, to be strengthened with might by his Spirit in the inner man* (Ephesians 3:16).[10]

For further information on how to be baptized in the Holy Spirit, read my booklet, *"I CAN Be Born Again and Spirit Filled,"* available through Marilyn Hickey Ministries for just $1.00.

Fruit of the Spirit

The purpose of a heritage of blessings in your family tree is so that you and your descendants can benefit from the good fruit or blessings promised by God in His Word. Both individually and as a family, the indwelling of the Holy Spirit enables you to uproot the family iniquities at work in your lives and bear spiritual fruit that will remain:

But the fruit of the Spirit, is love, joy, peace, longsuffering, gentleness, goodness, faith, Meekness, temperance: against such there is no law (Galatians 5:22,23).

All fruit has seed in it. Our fruit in the Spirit leaves seed for the next generation. Praise God that you can pass on good seed and fruit for your family to inherit. Although weeds from the evil tree may still come up from time to time (see chapter nine of this section for a further discussion of this), they will eventually be choked out by your spiritual fruit because the Word of God guarantees that "... *against such* [the fruit of the Spirit] *there is no law*" (Galatians 5:23).

Chapter Nine

HOW TO FACE THE ATTACK IF THE DEVIL COMES BACK

In chapter eight, we examined how to begin a heritage of blessings for your family tree. We discovered that depositing the Word of God in your own heart and in the hearts of your family members will provide power to purge the iniquities inherent in your bloodline and set you free to establish a pattern of covenant blessings.

If you'll recall in Matthew 13, Jesus tells the parable of the tares and wheat. He likens them to the types of seed that are planted and cultivated in a person's heart. He said that the seed, which is symbolic of the Word of God, was sown into good ground, but while the husbandman slept, the enemy came and sowed bad seed among the good. Thus, when the sower's seed began to sprout, the bad seed sprouted right alongside of the good:

> . . . *The kingdom of heaven is likened unto a man which*
> *sowed good seed in his field: But while men slept, his enemy*
> *came and sowed tares among the wheat, and went his way.*
> *But when the blade was sprung up, and brought forth fruit,*
> *then appeared the tares also. . . .* (Matthew 13:24-26).

Good seed and evil seed were planted in the hearts of your forefathers long before you were ever born, and it will take diligence to free your family tree of those stubborn weeds of sin. The tares and the wheat, the evil and the good, the curses and the blessings, grow side-by-side. As a result of Adam and Eve's transgression, you can't have one without the other. Even after you have broken the family curse and established generation blessings, you will still have to contend with the weeds—sins of your forefathers—that may resurface from time to time. Don't be alarmed, however; through the Word of God and the blood of Jesus, you can combat Satan and win.

Weeding Your Family Tree

I have a friend who pastors in a small town in a fairly large state. He and his wife have four sons and an adopted daughter. When his daughter turned 13, she became wild and began to slip out at night. Her school called and said she was creating a problem at school because she was trying to date boys, which her father did not want her to do because she was so young.

After he pondered the situation, he realized he'd never had that kind of problem with his two older sons. He began to fast and pray for his daughter, and asked God what was wrong and what he should do. The Lord spoke to him and said that he was dealing with a family iniquity or generation curse which was coming through the bloodline of his daughter's biological parents.

Living in a little town, he was able to trace her family tree. He knew his daughter's mother, and that she had given birth out of wedlock to his adopted daughter. He discovered that his daughter's biological mother and grandmother were also illegitimate. He prayed and bound the devil on behalf of his adopted daughter, but God told him that because his daughter was at the age of accountability, she would have to make the choice and bind the devil herself.

This man explained to his daughter that she was illegitimate, and that her mother and grandmother were illegitimate also. Then he told her that by the choices she was making, she was establishing a pattern of sin; it was very evident that she was following in her mother's and grandmother's footsteps and would probably get pregnant and have an illegitimate child, too.

"This is the devil's set-up for you," he explained to her. "Do you want God's divine destiny for you, or the devil's?"

This girl's father and mother had been diligent in training their children to serve the Lord. They had planted the seed of God's Word in this girl's heart, and at the time of her father's conversation with her, the Holy Spirit watered the Word that had been planted. Consequently, He gave her revelation of what her father was saying, and the girl chose to obey her father's instructions. (See chapter 8 for an in-depth look at the maturation process of a family tree.)

The girl understood immediately what her father was talking about. An evil spirit, familiar with her family's history of sexual sin, was trying to influence her to go the way of her forefathers. "Dad," she said, "I don't want to go that route." She repented and was cleansed of her biological family's iniquity. As a result, she was a virgin when she got married, and is still serving God today!

Familiar Spirits

In both the Old and New Testaments, God talks about familiar spirits. If you'll recall in I Samuel 28, Saul sought out a woman who had a familiar spirit to bring Samuel back from the dead. Instead of conjuring up Samuel's spirit, however, I believe the woman contacted a spirit that was familiar with Samuel's family tree:

> Then said Saul unto his servants, Seek me a woman that hath a familiar spirit, that I may go to her, and enquire of her. . . . Then said the woman, Whom shall I bring up unto thee? And he said, Bring me up Samuel (I Samuel 28:7,11).

Webster's Dictionary defines the word, *familiar,* as that "of a household, domestic; having to do with a family." In other words, a familiar spirit is one that is familiar with you and your family tree. It has followed your family line from generation to generation, and is intimately aware of and familiar with those hereditary weaknesses that run in your bloodline. It is equally aware of just how and when to plague you or your loved ones with the iniquities of the past. This is the mystery of iniquity referred to in II Thessalonians 2:7.

Satan has a host of demons dispatched to kill, steal, and destroy your family tree. These familiar spirits are assigned to follow each generation, and at the appropriate time, afflict them with these inherited weaknesses or tendencies. How sad to think that when a family member dies or is set free by the gospel of Jesus Christ, the familiar spirits that influenced him begin to search out others to afflict in his or the next generation.

You're probably thinking, "Marilyn, this is the most preposterous thing I've ever heard!" Matthew 12, however, bears witness to what I am saying:

> When the unclean spirit is gone out of a man, he walketh through dry places, seeking rest, and findeth none. Then he saith, **I will return into my house from whence I came out;** . . . (Matthew 12:43,44).

The word, *house,* is synonymous with "generation" in this passage of scripture. When you became born again, the curse of iniquity was broken in you and your future generations. The evil spirits that were accustomed to influencing and controlling you, no longer had authority over you because they were evicted from their place of residence. For example, as a Christian, I took authority over mental and emotional breakdowns in my life, my children's lives, and in my family tree. Although my father and grandfather both had nervous breakdowns, as a born-again believer, I inherited a new bloodline, the bloodline of Jesus Christ, Who has redeemed me from the curse of family iniquities.

This is where you need spiritual discernment, because although you are born-again and are free, these familiar spirits continue to hang around, waiting for a chance to repossess the house or family from which they were evicted.

The Greek translation of the word, *house,* is "a family." The unclean spirit is restless because it must inhabit a physical body. But because it can no longer influence you or cause you to walk in the way of your fathers, it says, "I know what I'll do. I'll return from the house or family tree from whence I came out."

This spirit will try to reenter a future generation. It will stalk your child or grandchild like a rapist does his victim. It will watch for the perfect timing—the right age or circumstance—to attack. If you used to smoke, drink, or take drugs, then it will watch for a certain age to tempt your child with the same thing.

The good news is you don't have to put up with Satan's tactics! You can stop him in his tracks and let him know that your family tree is off limits because God's covenant of generation blessings has been promised to you and your family, and it extends to a thousand generations:

> *Know therefore that the LORD thy God, he is God, the faithful God, which keepeth covenant and mercy with them that love him and keep his commandments to a thousand generations* (Deuteronomy 7:9).

Binding the Strong Man

"How," you may ask, "can I stop Satan in his tracks?" By disarming him! If you read of the wars in the Old Testament, you'll find many references to Israel spoiling their enemies' goods. To *spoil* means, "to plunder" or to take the property of another by force, to strip a person of their power and possessions:

> . . . *how can one enter into a strong man's house, and spoil his goods, except he first bind the strong man? and then he will spoil his house* (Matthew 12:29).

The strong man referred to in this text is the devil. You can bind him in your family tree just like my pastor friend tried to do for his daughter. But because she was of age, God said she had to bind, or prohibit the devil from operating in her family herself. No one could do it for her. James 4:7 says, *"Submit yourselves therefore to God. **Resist the devil, and he will flee from you.**"* Bind the devil in the name of Jesus. Each time you do this, you strip him of his power and his possessions—your family tree.

Regardless of what iniquities are in your background—drugs, sexual perversion, etc.—do your children a favor and be honest with them. Wait for the right age to warn them about the various things the devil may try to tempt them with and why; tell them it's a generation iniquity. Explain to them that you have repented of your past and have therefore been cleansed by the blood of Jesus. Therefore, you and your future generations are free, although the devil would like to reenter your bloodline through them.

If your children or grandchildren are already following a pattern of generation iniquity, then deal with them openly and honestly, like my pastor friend did. If you fail to act on this, and that familiar spirit is allowed to continue influencing them, the iniquity will become more and more of a stronghold and will increase in its intensity. What started out as anger in you, can develop into uncontrolled violence in your offspring, and murder in the next generation:

> . . . *and when he is come, he findeth it empty, swept, and garnished. Then goeth he, and taketh with himself, **seven other spirits more wicked than himself,** and they enter in and dwell there: and **the last state of that man is worse than the first**. . . .* (Matthew 12:44,45).

Perhaps you're beginning to see some things in your children that, after having read this chapter, are quite alarming. Don't be discouraged, however; the Word is bigger than your children and any generation iniquity. Keep it before you. Quote it to yourself, the devil, and your family. You may say, "I've made mistakes as a parent!" Well, so have a million other parents. I haven't met a perfect parent yet.

I have an adopted son who is in his thirties. He's not serving God yet, but he's going to. One time the devil told me, "You and your husband did this wrong and that wrong. As parents, you're failures!" You know how the devil can batter you.

I said, "Lord, I am so sorry." He said, "Marilyn, you've repented and repented over what you did wrong. You never acknowledge the good things you've done as a parent. I am the Father of Adam and Eve. Was I a good Father?"

I said, "Yes." He said, "Did Adam and Eve sin?" I said, "Yes." He said, "Whose fault was it? Mine or theirs?" I said, "Theirs."

Then he said, "I'm the Father of Israel. Was I a good Father?" I said, "You are a perfect Father." "Did Israel sin?" He asked. "Yes," I replied. "Whose fault was it, Mine or theirs?" I said, "Theirs."

God said, "Marilyn you carry the guilt of some things you should never carry. Adam, Eve, and Israel all made wrong choices, and I dealt with them and brought them through. Stop carrying the guilt of your son's choices. I Am that I Am, and I will bring him through, too."

Likewise, God will bring you and your family through to a place of victory and blessing in Him. Do not become alarmed or discouraged by the weeds that may poke through the soil of your loved ones' hearts from time to time. The Word and the blood of Jesus are working to cleanse your bloodline. Continue speaking and doing what it says, praising God that whom He has blessed, cannot be cursed (see Numbers 22:12).

Chapter Ten

WHEN YOU ARE WEAK...
THEN HE IS STRONG

God is a good God, and the devil is a bad devil. He doesn't give up his territory easily, nor will he take "No!" for an answer. In Luke 4, Satan tempted Jesus in the wilderness. After he failed, the Bible says he departed from Jesus *for a season.* The devil was foolish enough to believe that through his persistence, he could cause the Son of God to sin.

Satan will try the same tactic with you and your family; he will attempt to wear down and destroy your family tree. I once knew a pastor who loved God and was probably one of the most powerful pastors I have ever known. He was mightily used of God until he became involved in an affair with his secretary. This iniquity was passed to his two sons, who also became involved in sexual sin. Today, this pastor is no longer in the ministry.

What caused this man to fall? We know and understand from previous chapters that this was a family iniquity of sexual sin. This pastor didn't wake up one morning and say, "You know, today I'm going to ruin my life and that of my family's by having an affair with my secretary." No, it didn't happen like that. The familiar spirits that followed his family tree knew there was a family weakness to sexual sin. They watched and waited for just the right time to tempt this pastor and pressure him until he finally succumbed to the weakness he had inherited from his forefathers.

What this pastor did not realize, however, is that the moment he yielded in this area, he sold his sons as slaves on the sexual sin auction block. Had he resisted the temptation, the curse would have been reversed and the demons that tempted him would not have had such an easy inroad into the generation of his two sons. He could have established a family blessing.

I believe this pastor tried to resist the temptation to sin with his secretary in his own strength. Perhaps he was too embarrassed to share what was happening to him with a trusted friend. Or maybe he thought, "It'll never happen to me. I'm stronger than that!"

Tragically, because he gave in and allowed the sin to go unconfessed, a door was opened for the devil to come in and wreak havoc in this man's life and the lives of his descendants. If he had repented when the thoughts to commit adultery first occurred, then when the devil came to tempt him, he would have had God's strength to resist him. The devil would have had a hard time tempting him at all because he would not have been able to cross the bloodline of Jesus Christ.

In cleansing your bloodline and beginning a heritage of blessings for your family tree, I want you to know that the power of God is present to help you and you don't have to do it in your own strength. The Bible says that Jesus took your infirmities and bore your sicknesses. A simple definition of the word *infirmity* is an area of your life where you are not firm. For example, a person may not be firm in the area of his finances; he always spends his money foolishly. Someone else may not be firm in the area of their diet. He is overweight and constantly fighting the same battle to lose and/or maintain his weight.

Jesus took your infirmities, so, unlike my pastor friend, you don't have to try and resist the devil in your own strength. All you have to do is obey the Word in the area of finances or in the area(s) that you are unfirm. For example, Malachi 3 talks about the blessings that come with tithing. If you want to reverse the curse in the area of finances, then begin to tithe and give alms and offerings according to God's Word. By doing this, you are acknowledging that Jesus has paid the price, once and for all, and the area(s) in which you were unfirm become supernaturally strengthened.

The Faith Walk

In the previous chapter, we discovered that demonic spirits, known as familiar spirits, will stalk you and your family from generation to generation, looking for an opportunity to afflict you with your forefathers' sins. However, Jesus was bruised for your iniquities, and you don't have to take the devil's bruisings anymore. Jesus' blood has cleansed your family tree and you are free to produce good, healthy fruit in this and the next generation.

Second Corinthians 5:7 says, *"For we walk by faith, not by sight."* The Holy Spirit has reminded me of this many times. As a parent, as a pastor's wife, as founder and president of Marilyn Hickey Ministries, there have been times in my life where I have said to God, "I'm doing what your Word tells me to do, but . . . What am I doing wrong?"

"It's by faith, Marilyn," has been God's reply, "not sight."

Faith is simply acting as though the Word of God is true. Faith is thanking God for the answer *before* you receive the outward manifestation. Faith is ceasing from your own efforts to make your prayers work, and resting in the promises of His Word that it is already done. As I mentioned in chapter 9, I have an adopted son who is not yet serving the Lord, but I see his salvation through the eyes of faith— the Word of God promises it.

What I've shared with you in the pages of this book will have to be acted upon by faith. There will be times, for example, after you have followed the steps for cleansing your family tree and beginning a heritage of blessings, that things will become progressively worse. From time to time you may even wonder, "How much more can I take?" *Don't* throw in the towel! It is during these times that I want to assure you that you can rest in God's promises:

> . . . *God is not mocked: for whatsoever* [you] *soweth, that shall* [you] *also reap* (Galatians 6:7).

> . . . *Be not afraid nor dismayed by reason of this great multitude; for* **the battle is not your's, but God's** (II Chronicles 20:15).

When You Are Weak, Then You Are Strong

God's Word is His covenant, His contractual agreement with you that He cannot and will not break—He will do what the Bible says He will do. Of all the agreements, contracts, treaties, or pacts ever devised by man, none is more binding upon the parties involved than your covenant with God. It is based on His Son's shed blood, and is an exchange of Jesus' strength for your weaknesses.

When you became born again, Jesus took your weaknesses to the flesh in exchange for His supernatural ability and strength. Because of your covenant with Him, you and the members of your family tree are supernaturally empowered to overcome in areas of your life that up until the time of salvation, you had consistently failed in.

Through death, Jesus has become your strength. Through His death, came resurrection life. Through His shed blood, the very iniquities that have held you and your family bound, were rendered powerless:

> . . . *having canceled the written code, with its regulations, that was against us and that stood opposed to us; he took it away, nailing it to the cross. And having disarmed the powers and authorities, he made a public spectacle of them, triumphing over them by the cross* (Colossians 2:14,15 NIV).

The Apostle Paul understood the significance and purpose of his covenant with God. He realized that living the Christian life had nothing to do with his natural talents or abilities. It was Christ in him Who equipped and enabled him to do the supernatural. Paul's weaknesses were a source of joy to him because he knew that where his abilities ended, God's supernatural power began:

> *Therefore I take pleasure in infirmities, in reproaches, in necessities, in persecutions, in distresses for Christ's sake:* **for when I am weak, then am I strong** (II Corinthians 12:10).

Paul said, "I get happy when I'm weak. I get so happy when people talk about me, when I run out of money, when people persecute me, and throw rocks at me. I get so happy in distresses because when I am weak, then am I strong!"

"How," you might ask, "can a person become strong when they're weak?" The answer is simple: God's grace. It was sufficient for Paul and it is sufficient for you and the members of your family tree. *Grace* is God's unmerited favor, or His ability to "put you over" in any situation. It is a gift from God; you don't have to do anything short of salvation to receive it. Paul had a revelation of God's grace and understood how to rest in it.

In II Corinthians 12:9, Paul said he would glory in his infirmities so the power of God could rest upon him. The word, *infirmities*, is another word for "weaknesses." Had my pastor friend realized that where he was weak in the flesh, God's power could supernaturally strengthen him, then he may not have yielded to sexual sin.

How often do you depend on God's grace when you're in the throes of a difficult situation? When was the last time you were overcome with joy when your offspring, for the umpteenth time, yielded to that same family sin? Nehemiah 8:10 says the joy of the Lord is your strength, but I'm almost certain that few in the Body of Christ glory in their tribulations, or find an abundance of joy and peace during times of trouble.

Although Paul wrote two-thirds of the New Testament, and is considered by many as a great man of God, he understood his weakness in the flesh. Because of the abundance of revelations, he said he was given "... *a thorn in the flesh, the messenger of Satan to buffet me*, ... " (II Corinthians 12:7). Paul prayed to God three times to remove this thorn, but God's response was, "You can handle it, Paul. My power is resting upon you, giving you the strength you need in this situation":

> ... *My grace is sufficient for thee: for my strength is made perfect in weakness* ... (II Corinthians 12:9).

The word, *perfect*, in this passage of Scripture means, "to complete, consummate." God assured Paul that the thorn in his flesh was according to His will, that His grace would be provided to Paul to endure or suffer all things, and that Paul should learn to depend wholly upon the power of God so that His strength could be consummated or brought to full term in Paul's life.

You may think, "I'm weak. There's no way I can reverse the curse in my life, much less my family tree." But you can. First Corinthians 1:27 says God uses the weak things of this world to confound the mighty! Changing the tide of this and the next generation can only be done through God's grace. It will take His strength and not a man-made formula to weed the garden of your family tree, and to separate the tares from the wheat.

Establishing and maintaining a heritage of generation blessings is a supernatural act, not a natural one. It can only be accomplished in the spirit realm because the devil wants to permanently enslave the members of your family. Many Christians think that the devil can be overcome by following a few simple steps, but we know this is not the case. Because of the "mystery of iniquity" referred to in II Thessalonians 2:7, God's grace is the only key to overcoming generation iniquities—you must learn to rely on His power resting upon you and your future generations.

Don't major on your family's weaknesses or predispositions toward certain inherited sin. Imitate the Apostle Paul and glory in them, realizing that it is God's opportunity to perfect His strength in you. As you confess God's grace—His supernatural and perfected strength in your life—you will experience the power of His blood, that divine, supernatural cleansing agent, that Christ shed at Calvary to free you and your future generations from the curse of family iniquities.

Pray this prayer out loud and remind the devil that the blood of Jesus and God's grace is more than sufficient to maintain a heritage of blessings for your family tree:

Father, I thank You that Jesus Christ has given all we need to deliver us from every sin, trespass, and iniquity. The blood is enough. I declare these iniquities (name each iniquity), *and I repent of them and take the cleansing of the blood. Thank You that this bruise belongs to Jesus, Who was bruised for my iniquities. When the enemy tries to come, he will hit the blood. I will remind him that this part of my life that was weak is now strong because of God's grace and Jesus' blood, and the Spirit bears witness to the blood. The anointing is also there and the anointing has destroyed that yoke. In Jesus' name, Satan, you are defeated and you'll never destroy me or my household!*

Because of the blood of Jesus, you and your family are no longer victims of your past. The devil is defeated, and your best days are yet ahead. You have reversed the tide of family iniquities in your lives and are free to establish generations of blessings. Praise God NOW for victory for you, your children, and The NEXT Generation!

Chapter Eleven

PROMISES TO CLAIM FOR YOUR BLESSINGS TO REMAIN

Iniquity Scripture References

The following is a list of scripture references which correspond to the types of iniquities covered in this book. If you'll recall from chapter 2, an iniquity is a weakness, bend, or predisposition toward a certain behavior. As you search the Scriptures, you will discover that families, nations, the priesthood, and the land can all inherit a generation curse, which can only be broken through repentance, forgiveness, and the blood of Jesus.

Family Iniquity

And the serpent said unto the woman, Ye shall not surely die: For God doth know that in the day ye eat thereof, then your eyes shall be opened, and ye shall be as gods, knowing good and evil. And when the woman saw that the tree was good for food, and that it was pleasant to the eyes, and a tree to be desired to make one wise, she took of the fruit thereof, and did eat, and gave also unto her husband with her; and he did eat (Genesis 3:4-6).

*Thou shalt not bow down thyself to them, nor serve them: for I the LORD thy God am a jealous God, **visiting the iniquity of the fathers upon the children unto the third and fourth generations of them that hate me*** (Exodus 20:5).

And the goat shall bear upon him all their iniquities unto a land not inhabited: and he shall let go the goat in the wilderness (Leviticus 16:22).

. . . Who is David? . . . Shall I then take my bread, and my water, and my flesh that I have killed for my shearers, and give it unto men, whom I know not whence they be? (I Samuel 25:10,11).

Blessed is he whose transgression is forgiven, whose sin is covered. Blessed is the man unto whom the LORD imputeth not iniquity, and in whose spirit there is no guile. When I kept silence, my bones waxed old through my roaring all the day long. For day and night thy hand was heavy upon me: my moisture is turned into the drought of summer. . . . I acknowledged my sin unto thee, and mine iniquity have I not hid. I said, I will confess my transgressions unto the LORD; and thou forgavest the iniquity of my sin (Psalms 32:1-5).

Behold, I was shapen in iniquity; and in sin did my mother conceive me (Psalms 51:5).

Order my steps in thy word: and let not any iniquity have dominion over me (Psalms 119:133).

The words of a talebearer are as wounds, and they go down into the innermost parts of the belly (Proverbs 18:8).

As the bird by wandering, as the swallow by flying, so **the curse causeless shall not come** (Proverbs 26:2).

He that covereth his sins shall not prosper: but whoso confesseth and forsaketh them shall have mercy (Proverbs 28:13).

But he was wounded for our transgressions, he was bruised for our iniquities: the chastisement of our peace was upon him; **and with his stripes we are healed** (Isaiah 53:5).

. . . and when he is come, he findeth it empty, swept, and garnished. Then goeth he, and taketh with himself, **seven other spirits more wicked than himself,** *and they enter in and dwell there: and* **the last state of that man is worse than the first. . . .** (Matthew 12:44,45).

Forgive us our debts, as we have also forgiven our debtors. For if you forgive men when they sin against you, your heavenly Father will also forgive you (Matthew 6:12,14 NIV).

When the unclean spirit is gone out of a man, he walketh through dry places, seeking rest, and findeth none. Then he saith, **I will return into my house from whence I came out;** *. . .* (Matthew 12:43,44).

And because iniquity shall abound, the love of many shall wax cold (Matthew 24:12).

And there was there an herd of many swine feeding on the mountain: and they besought him that he would suffer them to enter into them. And he suffered them. Then went the devils out of the man, and entered into the swine: and the herd ran violently down a steep place into the lake, and were choked (Luke 8:32,33).

Now this man purchased a field with the reward of iniquity; and falling headlong, he burst asunder in the midst, and all his bowels gushed out (Acts 1:18).

And when Simon saw that through laying on of the apostles' hands the Holy Ghost was given, he offered them money, Saying, Give me also this power, that on whomsoever I lay hands, he may receive the Holy Ghost. But Peter said unto him, Thy money perish with thee, because thou hast thought that the gift of God may be purchased with money. For I perceive that thou art in the gall of bitterness, and in the bond of iniquity (Acts 8:18,19,23).

*. . . Hearing ye shall hear, and shall not understand; and seeing ye shall see, and not perceive: For **the heart of this people is waxed gross,** and their ears are dull of hearing, **and their eyes have they closed;** lest they should see with their eyes, and hear with their ears, and understand with their heart, and should be converted, and I should heal them* (Acts 28:26,27).

*Therefore thou art inexcusable, O man, whosoever thou art that judgest: for wherein thou judgest another, thou condemnest thyself; **for thou that judgest doest the same things*** (Romans 2:1).

For all have sinned, and come short of the glory of God (Romans 3:23).

Wherefore, as by one man sin entered into the world, and death by sin; and so death passed upon all men, for that all have sinned (Romans 5:12).

Know ye not, that to whom ye yield yourselves servants to obey, his servants ye are to whom ye obey; whether of sin unto death, or of obedience unto righteousness? (Romans 6:16).

. . . know ye not that he which is joined to an harlot is one body? for two, saith he, shall be one flesh. . . . Every sin that a man doeth is without the body; but he that committeth fornication sinneth against his own body (I Corinthians 6:16,18).

For sin shall not have dominion over you: . . . ye were the servants of sin, but ye have obeyed from the heart . . . Being then made free from sin, . . . For the wages of sin is death; but the gift of God is eternal life through Jesus Christ our Lord (Romans 6:14,17,18,23).

For he had made him to be sin for us, who knew no sin; that we might be made the righteousness of God in him (II Corinthians 5:21).

Neither give place to the devil (Ephesians 4:27).

For the mystery of iniquity doth already work: . . . (II Thessalonians 2:7).

Who gave himself for us, that he might **redeem us from all iniquity, and purify unto himself a peculiar people, zealous of good works** (Titus 2:14).

But if we walk in the light, as he is in the light, we have fellowship one with another, **and the blood of Jesus Christ his Son cleanseth us from all sin.** *If we say that we have no sin, we deceive ourselves, and the truth is not in us. If we confess our sins, he is faithful and just to forgive us our sins, and to cleanse us from all unrighteousness* (I John 1:7-9).

. . . For this purpose the Son of God was manifested, that he might destroy the works of the devil [in your life] (I John 3:8).

National Iniquity

To the woman he said, I will greatly increase your pains in childbearing; with pain you will give birth to children . . . (Genesis 3:16 NIV).

. . . the iniquity of the Amorites is not yet full (Genesis 15:16).

And Abraham drew near, and said, Wilt thou also destroy the righteous with the wicked? Peradventure there be fifty righteous within the city: wilt thou also destroy and not spare the place for the fifty righteous that are therein? And the LORD said, If I find . . . fifty righteous within the city, then I will spare all the place for their sakes. . . . Peradventure ten shall be found there. And he said, I will not destroy it for ten's sake (Genesis 18:23,24,26,32).

And the goat shall bear upon him all their iniquities unto a land not inhabited: and he shall let go the goat in the wilderness (Leviticus 16:22).

If they shall confess their iniquity, and the iniquity of their fathers, with their trespass which they trespassed against me, and that also they have walked contrary unto me; And that I also have walked contrary unto them, and have brought them into the land of their enemies; if then their uncircumcised hearts be humbled, and they then accept of the punishment of their iniquity, Then will I remember my covenant . . . and I will remember the land (Leviticus 26:40-42).

But of the cities of these people, which the LORD thy God doth give thee for an inheritance, thou shalt save alive nothing that breatheth: But thou shalt utterly destroy them; . . . (Deuteronomy 20:16,17).

Then said Saul unto his servants, Seek me a woman that hath a familiar spirit, that I may go to her, and enquire of her. . . . Then said the woman, Whom shall I bring up unto thee? And he said, Bring me up Samuel (I Samuel 28:7,11).

But king Solomon loved many strange women, together with the daughter of Pharaoh, women of the Moabites, Ammonites, Edomites, Zidonians, and Hittites; Of the nations concerning which the LORD said unto the children of Israel, Ye shall not go in to them, neither shall they come in unto you: for surely they will turn your heart after their gods: . . . And he had seven hundred wives, princesses, and three hundred concubines: . . . For it came to pass, when Solomon was old, that his wives turned away his heart after other gods: . . . (I Kings 11:1-4).

*And Rehoboam the son of Solomon reigned in Judah. . . . And Judah did evil in the sight of the LORD, and they provoked him to jealousy with their sins which they had committed, above all that their **fathers had done.** For they also built them high places, and images, and groves, on every high hill, and under every green tree. Now in the eighteenth year of king Jeroboam the son of Nebat reigned Abijam* *over Judah. And **he walked in all the sins of his father, which he had done before him:** . . .* (I Kings 14:21-23; 15:1,3).

And Joshua, and all Israel with him, took Achan the son of Zerah, and the silver, and the garment, and the wedge of gold, and his sons, and his daughters, and his oxen, and his asses, and his sheep, and his tent, and all that he had: and they brought them unto the valley of Achor. . . . And all Israel stoned him with stones, and burned them with fire, after they had stoned them with stones (Joshua 7:24,25).

If my people, which are called by my name, shall humble themselves, and pray, and seek my face, and turn from their wicked ways; then will I hear from heaven, and will forgive their sin, and will heal their land (II Chronicles 7:14).

*. . . I beseech thee, O LORD God of heaven, the great and terrible God, that keepeth covenant and mercy for them that love him and observe his commandments: Let thine ear now be attentive, and thine eyes open, that thou mayest hear the prayer of thy servant, which I pray before thee now, day and night, for the children of Israel thy servants, and confess the sins of the children of Israel, which we have sinned against thee: both **I and my father's house have sinned*** (Nehemiah 1:5,6).

*And the seed of Israel separated themselves from all strangers, and stood and **confessed their sins, and the iniquities of their fathers*** (Nehemiah 9:2).

Ah sinful nation, a people laden with iniquity, a seed of evildoers, children that are corrupters: they have forsaken the LORD, they have provoked the Holy One of Israel unto anger, they are gone away backward (Isaiah 1:4).

We acknowledge, O LORD, our wickedness, and the iniquity of our fathers: for we have sinned against thee (Jeremiah 14:20).

Our fathers have sinned and are not; and we have borne their iniquities (Lamentations 5:7).

And to the others he said in mine hearing, Go ye after him through the city, and smite: let not your eye spare, neither have ye pity: Slay utterly old and young, both maids, and little children, and women: but come not near any man upon whom is the mark; and begin at my sanctuary. Then they began at the ancient men which were before the house. And he said unto them, Defile the house, and fill the courts with the slain: go ye forth. And they went forth, and slew in the city (Ezekiel 9:5-7).

Then said he unto me, The iniquity of the house of Israel and Judah is exceeding great, and the land is full of blood, and the city full of perverseness: for they say, The LORD hath forsaken the earth, and the LORD seeth not. And as for me also, mine eye shall not spare, neither will I have pity, but I will recompense their way upon their head (Ezekiel 9:9,10).

. . . O Lord, the great and dreadful God, keeping the covenant and mercy to them that love him, and to them that keep his commandments; **We have sinned, and have committed iniquity,** *and have done wickedly, and have rebelled, even by departing from thy precepts and from thy judgments* (Daniel 9:4,5).

We have sinned, and have committed iniquity, and have done wickedly, . . . because for our sins, and for the iniquities of our fathers, Jerusalem and thy people are become a reproach to all that are about us (Daniel 9:5,16).

. . . while I was still in prayer, **Gabriel, the man I had seen in the earlier vision, came to me in swift flight about the time of the evening sacrifice. He instructed me . . . As soon as you began to pray, an answer was given,** *which I have come to tell you, . . . Seventy 'sevens' are decreed for your people and your holy city to finish transgression, to put an end to sin, to atone for wickedness, to bring in everlasting righteousness, to seal up vision and prophecy and to anoint the most holy* (Daniel 9:21-24 NIV)

If we confess our sins, he is faithful and just to forgive us of our sins, and to **cleanse** *us from all unrighteousness* (I John 1:9).

Priestly Iniquity

And it came to pass, as he [Moses] *had made an end of speaking all these words, that the ground clave asunder that was under them: And the earth opened her mouth, and swallowed them up, and their houses, and all the men that appertained unto Korah, and all their goods* (Numbers 16:31,32).

Blessed is he whose transgression is forgiven, whose sin is covered. Blessed is the man unto whom the LORD imputeth not iniquity, and in whose spirit there is no guile. When I kept silence, my bones waxed old through my roaring all the day long. For day and night thy hand was heavy upon me: my moisture is turned into the drought of summer. . . . I acknowledged my sin unto thee, and mine iniquity have I not hid. I said, I will confess my transgressions unto the LORD; and thou forgavest the iniquity of my sin (Psalms 32:1-5).

Land Iniquity

. . . Cursed is the ground because of you; through painful toil you will eat of it all the days of your life. It will produce thorns and thistles for you, and you will eat the plants of the field. By the sweat of your brow you will eat your food . . . (Genesis 3:17,18 NIV).

If they shall confess their iniquity, and the iniquity of their fathers, with their trespass which they trespassed against me, and that also they have walked contrary unto me; And that I also have walked contrary unto them, and have brought them into the land of their enemies; if then their uncircumcised hearts be humbled, and they then accept of the punishment of their iniquity, Then will I remember my covenant . . . and I will remember the land (Leviticus 26:40-42).

. . . Upon me, my lord, upon me let this iniquity be . . . forgive the trespass of thine handmaid: for the LORD will certainly make my lord a sure house; because my lord fighteth the battles of the LORD, and evil hath not been found in thee all thy days (I Samuel 25:24,28).

If my people, which are called by my name, shall humble themselves, and pray, and seek my face, and turn from their wicked ways; then will I hear from heaven, and will forgive their sin, and will heal their land (II Chronicles 7:14).

Blessing Scripture References

The Blessing: Divine Health
He sent his word, and healed them, and delivered them from their destructions (Psalms 107:20).

Surely he hath borne our griefs, and carried our sorrows: . . . But he was wounded for our transgressions, he was bruised for our iniquities: the chastisement of our peace was upon him; and with his stripes we are healed (Isaiah 53:4,5).

. . . let the weak say, I am strong (Joel 3:10).

Beloved, I wish above all things that thou mayest prosper and be in health, even as thy soul prospereth (III John 2).

Who his own self bare our sins in his own body on the tree, that we, being dead to sins, should live unto righteousness: by whose stripes ye were healed (I Peter 2:24).

Be not wise in thine own eyes: fear the LORD, and depart from evil. It shall be health to thy navel, and marrow to thy bones (Proverbs 3:7,8).

The Blessing: Fidelity
Marriage is honourable in all, and the bed undefiled: but whoremongers and adulterers God will judge (Hebrews 13:4).

. . . reproofs of instruction are the way of life: To keep thee from the evil woman, from the flattery of the tongue of a strange woman. Lust not after her beauty in thine heart; . . . (Proverbs 6:23-25).

The Blessing: Freedom from Alcohol
O taste and see that the LORD is good: blessed is the man that trusteth in him (Psalms 34:8).

. . . If any man thirst, let him come unto me, and drink (John 7:37).

Jesus answered and said unto her, Whosoever drinketh of this water shall thirst again: But whosoever drinketh of the water that I shall give him shall never thirst; but the water that I shall give him shall be in him a well of water springing up into everlasting life (John 4:13,14).

Then they cried unto the LORD in their trouble, and he delivered them out of their distresses (Psalms 107:6).

And it shall come to pass, that whosoever shall call on the name of the LORD shall be delivered: . . . (Joel 2:32).

If the Son therefore shall make you free, ye shall be free indeed (John 8:36).

For the law of the Spirit of life in Christ Jesus hath made me free from the law of sin and death (Romans 8:2).

The Blessing: Freedom from Arthritis
Behold, thou hast instructed many, and thou hast strengthened the weak hands. Thy words have upholden him that was falling, and thou hast strengthened the feeble knees (Job 4:3,4).

Wherefore lift up the hands which hang down, and the feeble knees; And make straight paths for your feet, lest that which is lame be turned out of the way; but let it rather be healed (Hebrews 12:12,13).

The Blessing: Freedom from Asthma and Colds
Why art thou cast down, O my soul? and why art thou disquieted within me? hope thou in God: for I shall yet praise him, who is the health of my countenance, and my God (Psalms 42:11).

. . . seeing he giveth to all life, and breath, and all things (Acts 17:25).

The Blessing: A Soft Tongue
How forcible are right words! but what doth your arguing reprove? (Job 6:25).

The Blessing: Freedom from Back Pain
The LORD upholdeth all that fall, and raiseth up all those that be bowed down (Psalms 145:14).

The Blessing: Steadfastness

These things have I written unto you that believe on the name of the Son of God; that ye may know that ye have eternal life, . . . (I John 5:13).

. . . I know whom I have believed, and am persuaded that he is able to keep that which I have committed unto him against that day (II Timothy 1:12).

Hereby know we that we dwell in him, and he in us, because he hath given us of his Spirit (I John 4:13).

The Spirit itself beareth witness with our spirit, that we are the children of God (Romans 8:16).

The Blessing: Freedom from Blood Disease (Leukemia, Abnormal Blood Pressure, Diabetes)

. . . I said unto thee when thou wast in thy blood, Live; yea, I said unto thee when thou wast in thy blood, Live (Ezekiel 16:6).

Behold, I will bring it health and cure, and I will cure them, and will reveal unto them the abundance of peace and truth (Jeremiah 33:6).

Confess your faults one to another, and pray one for another, that ye may be healed. The effectual fervent prayer of a righteous man availeth much (James 5:16).

For I will cleanse their blood that I have not cleansed: . . . (Joel 3:21).

The Blessing: Freedom from Bone Disease

Pleasant words are as an honeycomb, sweet to the soul, and health to the bones (Proverbs 16:24).

Have mercy upon me, O LORD; for I am weak: O LORD, heal me; for my bones are vexed (Psalms 6:2).

The Blessing: Strong, Healthy Bones

He keepeth all his bones: not one of them is broken (Psalms 34:20).

The Blessing: Freedom from Burns

. . . when thou walkest through the fire, thou shalt not be burned; neither shall the flame kindle upon thee (Isaiah 43:2).

. . . the LORD is thy shade upon thy right hand. The sun shall not smite thee by day, nor the moon by night (Psalms 121:5,6).

The Blessing: Freedom from Cancer

For verily I say unto you, That whosoever shall say unto this mountain, Be thou removed, and be thou cast into the sea; and shall not doubt in his heart, but shall believe that those things which he saith shall come to pass; he shall have whatsoever he saith. Therefore I say unto you, What things soever ye desire, when ye pray, believe that ye receive them, and ye shall have them (Mark 11:23,24).

. . . Every plant, which my heavenly Father hath not planted, shall be rooted up (Matthew 15:13).

The Blessing: No Condemnation

There is therefore now no condemnation to them which are in Christ Jesus, . . . (Romans 8:1).

The Blessing: Freedom from Demonic Attacks

Wherefore take unto you the whole armour of God, that ye may be able to withstand in the evil day, and having done all, to stand. Stand therefore, having your loins girt about with truth, and having on the breastplate of righteousness; And your feet shod with the preparation of the gospel of peace; Above all, taking the shield of faith, wherewith ye shall be able to quench all the fiery darts of the wicked. And take the helmet of salvation, and the sword of the Spirit, which is the word of God: Praying always with all prayer and supplication in the Spirit, . . . (Ephesians 6:13-18).

The Blessing: Honesty

Providing for honest things, not only in the sight of the Lord, but also in the sight of men (II Corinthians 8:21).

Neither give place to the devil (Ephesians 4:27).

Recompense to no man evil for evil. Provide things honest in the sight of all men (Romans 12:17).

Create in me a clean heart, O God; and renew a right spirit within me (Psalms 51:10).

The Blessing: Healthy Eyes and Ears
The LORD openeth the eyes of the blind: . . . (Psalms 146:8).

And the eyes of them that see shall not be dim, and the ears of them that hear shall hearken (Isaiah 32:3).

And in that day shall the deaf hear the words of the book, and the eyes of the blind shall see out of obscurity, and out of darkness (Isaiah 29:18).

Then the eyes of the blind shall be opened, and the ears of the deaf shall be unstopped (Isaiah 35:5).

The blind receive their sight, . . . and the deaf hear, . . . (Matthew 11:5).

The Blessing: Endurance
He giveth power to the faint; and to them that have no might he increaseth strength. But they that wait upon the LORD shall renew their strength; . . . (Isaiah 40:29,31).

Though I walk in the midst of trouble, thou wilt revive me: thou shalt stretch forth thine hand . . . and thy right hand shall save me (Psalms 138:7).

. . . but the spirit giveth life (II Corinthians 3:6).

The Blessing: Boldness
I can do all things through Christ which strengtheneth me (Philippians 4:13).

. . . greater is he that is in you, than he that is in the world (I John 4:4).

But ye shall receive power, after that the Holy Ghost is come upon you: and ye shall be witnesses unto me . . . (Acts 1:8).

The wicked flee when no man pursueth: but the righteous are bold as a lion (Proverbs 28:1).

. . . the people that do know their God shall be strong, and do exploits (Daniel 11:32).

The Blessing: Courage
Nay, in all these things we are more than conquerors through him that loved us (Romans 8:37).

In God I will praise his word, in God I have put my trust; I will not fear what flesh can do unto me (Psalms 56:4).

The Blessing: Freedom from Fear of Old Age
Bless the LORD, O my soul: and all that is within me, bless his holy name. Bless the LORD, O my soul, and forget not all his benefits: Who forgiveth all thine iniquities; who healeth all thy diseases; Who redeemeth thy life from destruction; who crowneth thee with lovingkindness and tender mercies; Who satisfieth thy mouth with good things; so that thy youth is renewed like the eagle's (Psalms 103:1-5).

The righteous . . . shall still bring forth fruit in old age; they shall be fat and flourishing (Psalms 92:12,14).

The Blessing: Freedom from Feet Trouble
For thou hast delivered my soul from death, mine eyes from tears, and my feet from falling. I will walk before the LORD in the land of the living (Psalms 116:8,9).

Then shalt thou walk in thy way safely, and thy foot shall not stumble (Proverbs 3:23).

The Blessing: A Wise Tongue
Whoso keepeth his mouth and his tongue keepeth his soul from troubles (Proverbs 21:23).

For he that will love life, and see good days, let him refrain his tongue from evil, and his lips that they speak no guile (I Peter 3:10).

He that hath knowledge spareth his words: . . . (Proverbs 17:27).

In the multitude of words there wanteth not sin: but he that refraineth his lips is wise (Proverbs 10:19).

A man hath joy by the answer of his mouth: and a word spoken in due season, how good is it! (Proverbs 15:23).

Let no corrupt communication proceed out of your mouth, but that which is good to the use of edifying, that it may minister grace unto the hearers (Ephesians 4:29).

Let your speech be alway with grace, seasoned with salt, that ye may know how ye ought to answer every man (Colossians 4:6).

Set a watch, O LORD, before my mouth; keep the door of my lips (Psalms 141:3).

The Blessing: Wisdom
But of him are ye in Christ Jesus, who of God is made unto us wisdom, . . . (I Corinthians 1:30).

The Blessing: Strong Hands
Strengthen ye the weak hands, and confirm the feeble knees (Isaiah 35:3).

The Blessing: Walking in Love
. . . love one another; as I have loved you, that ye also love one another (John 13:34).

. . . the love of God is shed abroad in our hearts by the Holy Ghost . . . (Romans 5:5).

The Blessing: Freedom from Headaches and Migraines
But if the Spirit of him that raised up Jesus from the dead dwell in you, he that raised up Christ from the dead shall also quicken your mortal bodies by his Spirit that dwelleth in you (Romans 8:11).

This is my comfort in my affliction: for thy word hath quickened me (Psalms 119:50).

The Blessing: A Healthy Heart

Wait on the LORD: be of good courage, and he shall strengthen thine heart: wait, I say, on the LORD (Psalms 27:14).

The LORD is my strength and my shield; my heart trusted in him, and I am helped: therefore my heart greatly rejoiceth; and with my song will I praise him (Psalms 28:7).

Be of good courage, and he shall strengthen your heart, all ye that hope in the LORD (Psalms 31:24).

Keep thy heart with all diligence; for out of it are the issues of life (Proverbs 4:23).

A merry heart doeth good like a medicine: but a broken spirit drieth the bones (Proverbs 17:22).

The Blessing: Self Confidence

. . . yet not I, but Christ liveth in me: . . . (Galatians 2:20).

. . . I know whom I have believed, and am persuaded that he is able . . . (II Timothy 1:12).

. . . If God be for us, who can be against us? (Romans 8:31).

So that we may boldly say, The Lord is my helper, and I will not fear what man shall do unto me (Hebrews 13:6).

Not that we are sufficient of ourselves to think any thing as of ourselves; but our sufficiency is of God (II Corinthians 3:5).

Whoso offereth praise glorifieth me: . . . (Psalms 50:23).

Giving thanks always for all things unto God and the Father in the name of our Lord Jesus Christ (Ephesians 5:20).

By him therefore let us offer the sacrifice of praise to God continually, . . . (Hebrews 13:15).

In every thing give thanks: for this is the will of God in Christ Jesus concerning you (I Thessalonians 5:18).

As ye have therefore received Christ Jesus the Lord, so walk ye in him: Rooted and built up in him, and stablished in the faith, as ye have been taught, abounding therein with thanksgiving (Colossians 2:6,7).

The Blessing: Fertility

. . . there shall not be male or female barren among you, . . . (Deuteronomy 7:14).

He maketh the barren woman to keep house, and to be a joyful mother of children . . . (Psalms 113:9).

The Blessing: Sweet Sleep

I will both lay me down in peace, and sleep: for thou, LORD, only makest me dwell in safety (Psalms 4:8).

It is vain for you to rise up early, to sit up late, to eat the bread of sorrows: for so he giveth his beloved sleep (Psalms 127:2).

For the LORD hath poured out upon you the spirit of deep sleep, and hath closed your eyes: . . . (Isaiah 29:10).

When thou liest down, thou shalt not be afraid: yea, thou shalt lie down, and thy sleep shall be sweet (Proverbs 3:24).

The Blessing: Faith

. . . God hath dealt to every man the measure of faith (Romans 12:3).

The Blessing: Mental Health

In the multitude of my thoughts within me thy comforts delight my soul (Psalms 94:19).

The LORD also will be a refuge for the oppressed, a refuge in times of trouble (Psalms 9:9).

Commit thy works unto the LORD, and thy thoughts shall be established (Proverbs 16:3).

. . . But we have the mind of Christ (I Corinthians 2:16).

Casting down imaginations, and every high thing that exalteth itself against the knowledge of God, and bringing into captivity every thought to the obedience of Christ (II Corinthians 10:5).

And the peace of God, which passeth all understanding, shall keep your hearts and minds through Christ Jesus (Philippians 4:7).

For God hath not given us the spirit of fear; but of power, and of love, and of a sound mind (II Timothy 1:7).

The Blessing: Freedom from Mouth, Lip, Tongue Problems
Whoso keepeth his mouth and his tongue keepeth his soul from troubles (Proverbs 21:23).

And straightway his ears were opened, and the string of his tongue was loosed, and he spake plain. And [they] *were beyond measure astonished, saying, He hath done all things well: he maketh both the deaf to hear, and the dumb to speak* (Mark 7:35,37).

The mouth of a righteous man is a well of life: . . . (Proverbs 10:11).

He that keepeth his mouth keepeth his life: but he that openeth wide his lips shall have destruction (Proverbs 13:3).

The Blessing: Freedom from Muscular Dystropy and Multiple Sclerosis
There shall no evil befall thee, neither shall any plague come nigh thy dwelling. For he shall give his angels charge over thee, to keep thee in all thy ways. They shall bear thee up in their hands, lest thou dash thy foot against a stone (Psalms 91:10-12).

The Blessing: Positive Self-image
Do ye look on things after the outward appearance? If any man trust to himself that he is Christ's, let him of himself think this again, that, as he is Christ's, even so are we Christ's (II Corinthians 10:7).

Herein is our love made perfect, that we may have boldness in the day of judgment: because as he is, so are we in this world (I John 4:17).

The Blessing: Calm Nerves
God is our refuge and strength, a very present help in trouble (Psalms 46:1).

Cast thy burden upon the LORD, and he shall sustain thee: he shall never suffer the righteous to be moved (Psalms 55:22).

. . . where the Spirit of the Lord is, there is liberty (II Corinthians 3:17).

The Blessing: Freedom from Occult Practices
Wherefore God also hath highly exalted him, and given him a name which is above every name: That at the name of Jesus every knee should bow, of things in heaven, and things in earth, and things under the earth: And that every tongue should confess that Jesus Christ is Lord, to the glory of God the Father (Philippians 2:9-11).

Submit yourselves therefore to God. Resist the devil, and he will flee from you (James 4:7).

Lest Satan should get an advantage of us: for we are not ignorant of his devices (II Corinthians 2:11).

Behold, I give unto you power to tread on serpents and scorpions, and over all the power of the enemy: and nothing shall by any means hurt you (Luke 10:19).

. . . When the enemy shall come in like a flood, the spirit of the LORD shall lift up a standard against him (Isaiah 59:19).

And ought not this woman, being a daughter of Abraham, whom Satan hath bound, lo, these eighteen years, be loosed from this bond on the sabbath day? (Luke 13:16).

Put on the whole armour of God, that ye may be able to stand against the wiles of the devil. For we wrestle not against flesh and blood, but against principalities, against powers, against the rulers of the darkness of this world, against spiritual wickedness in high places (Ephesians 6:11,12).

The Blessing: Freedom from Oppression
Stand fast therefore in the liberty wherewith Christ hath made us free, and be not entangled again with the yoke of bondage (Galatians 5:1).

And it shall come to pass in that day, that his burden shall be taken away from off thy shoulder, and his yoke from off thy neck, and the yoke shall be destroyed because of the anointing (Isaiah 10:27).

The LORD is my light and my salvation; whom shall I fear? the LORD is the strength of my life; of whom shall I be afraid? (Psalms 27:1).

If the Son therefore shall make you free, ye shall be free indeed (John 8:36).

The Blessing: Freedom from Palsy and Strokes
Thy vows are upon me, O God: I will render praises unto thee. For thou hast delivered my soul from death: wilt not thou deliver my feet from falling, that I may walk before God in the light of the living? (Psalms 56:12,13).

The Blessing: Preservation
They shall take up serpents; and if they drink any deadly thing, it shall not hurt them; . . . (Mark 16:18).

Thou hast clothed me with skin and flesh, and hast fenced me with bones and sinews. Thou hast granted me life and favour, and thy visitation hath preserved my spirit (Job 10:11).

The Blessing: Prosperity
But my God shall supply all your need according to his riches in glory by Christ Jesus (Philippians 4:19).

This book of the law shall not depart out of thy mouth; but thou shalt meditate therein day and night, that thou mayest observe to do according to all that is written therein: for then thou shalt make thy way prosperous, and then thou shalt have good success (Joshua 1:8).

Blessed is the man that walketh not in the counsel of the ungodly, nor standeth in the way of sinners, nor sitteth in the seat of the scornful.

But his delight is in the law of the LORD; and in his law doth he meditate day and night. And he shall be like a tree planted by the rivers of water, that bringeth forth his fruit in his season; his leaf also shall not wither; and whatsoever he doeth shall prosper (Psalms 1:1-3).

But seek ye first the kingdom of God, and his righteousness; and all these things shall be added unto you (Matthew 6:33).

But thou shalt remember the LORD thy God: for it is he that giveth thee power to get wealth, . . . (Deuteronomy 8:18).

Beloved, I wish above all things that thou mayest prosper and be in health, even as thy soul prospereth (III John 2).

The thief cometh not, but for to steal, and to kill, and to destroy: I am come that they might have life, and that they might have it more abundantly (John 10:10).

Honour the LORD with thy substance, and with the firstfruits of all thine increase: So shall thy barns be filled with plenty, and thy presses shall burst out with new wine (Proverbs 3:9,10).

Give, and it shall be given unto you; good measure, pressed down, and shaken together, and running over, shall men give into your bosom. For with the same measure that ye mete withal it shall be measured to you again (Luke 6:38).

Beloved, if our heart condemn us not, then have we confidence toward God. And whatsoever we ask, we receive of him, because we keep his commandments, and do those things that are pleasing in his sight (I John 3:21,22).

The Blessing: Freedom from Profanity
But now ye also put off all these; anger, wrath, malice, blasphemy, filthy communication out of your mouth (Colossians 3:8).

Pleasant words are as an honeycomb, sweet to the soul, and health to the bones (Proverbs 16:24).

Death and life are in the power of the tongue: and they that love it shall eat the fruit thereof (Proverbs 18:21).

A wholesome tongue is a tree of life: . . . (Proverbs 15:4).

The Blessing: Obedient Children
My son, attend to my words; incline thine ear unto my sayings. Let them not depart from thine eyes; keep them in the midst of thine heart. For they are life unto those that find them, and health to all their flesh (Proverbs 4:20-22).

Thus saith the LORD; Refrain thy voice from weeping, and thine eyes from tears: for thy work shall be rewarded, saith the LORD; and they shall come again from the land of the enemy (Jeremiah 31:16).

The Blessing: Joy
Thou wilt shew me the path of life: in thy presence is fullness of joy; at thy right hand there are pleasures for evermore (Psalms 16:11).

Then he said unto them, Go your way, eat the fat, and drink the sweet, and send portions unto them for whom nothing is prepared: for this day is holy unto our Lord: neither be ye sorry; for the joy of the LORD is your strength (Nehemiah 8:10).

And ye now therefore have sorrow: but I will see you again, and your heart shall rejoice, and your joy no man taketh from you (John 16:22).

Whom having not seen, ye love; in whom, though now ye see him not, yet believing, ye rejoice with joy unspeakable and full of glory (I Peter 1:8).

But none of these things move me, neither count I my life dear unto myself, so that I might finish my course with joy, . . . (Acts 20:24).

This is the day which the LORD hath made; we will rejoice and be glad in it (Psalms 118:24).

Make a joyful noise unto the LORD, all ye lands. Serve the LORD with gladness: come before his presence with singing. Know ye that the LORD he is God: it is he that hath made us, and not we ourselves; we are his people, and the sheep of his pasture. Enter into his gates with thanksgiving, and into his courts with praise: be thankful unto him, and bless his name. For the LORD is good; his mercy is everlasting; and his truth endureth to all generations (Psalms 100:1-5).

A merry heart maketh a cheerful countenance: but by sorrow of the heart the spirit is broken (Proverbs 15:13).

Fear thou not; for I am with thee: be not dismayed; for I am thy God: I will strengthen thee; yea, I will help thee; yea, I will uphold thee with the right hand of my righteousness (Isaiah 41:10).

The Blessing: Generosity
For God so loved the world, that he gave his only begotten Son, that whosoever believeth in him should not perish, but have everlasting life (John 3:16).

. . . It is more blessed to give than to receive (Acts 20:35).

Will a man rob God? Yet ye have robbed me. But ye say, Wherein have we robbed thee? In tithes and offerings. Ye are cursed with a curse: for ye have robbed me, even this whole nation. Bring ye all the tithes into the storehouse, that there may be meat in mine house, and prove me now herewith, saith the LORD of hosts, if I will not open you the windows of heaven, and pour you out a blessing, that there shall not be room enough to receive it. And I will rebuke the devourer for your sakes, and he shall not destroy the fruits of your ground; neither shall your vine cast her fruit before the time in the field, saith the LORD of hosts. And all nations shall call you blessed: for ye shall be a delightsome land, saith the LORD of hosts (Malachi 3:8-12).

There is that scattereth, and yet increaseth; and there is that withholdeth more than is meet, but it tendeth to poverty (Proverbs 11:24).

But this I say, He which soweth sparingly shall reap also sparingly; and he which soweth bountifully shall reap also bountifully. Every man according as he purposeth in his heart, so let him give; not grudgingly, or of necessity: for God loveth a cheerful giver (II Corinthians 9:6,7).

The Blessing: Self-assuredness
The fear of man bringeth a snare: but whoso putteth his trust in the LORD shall be safe (Proverbs 29:25).

The Blessing: Freedom from Addictions
He hath delivered my soul in peace from the battle that was against me: . . . (Psalms 55:18).

For I the LORD thy God will hold thy right hand, saying unto thee, Fear not; I will help thee (Isaiah 41:13).

Know ye not that ye are the temple of God, and that the Spirit of God dwelleth in you? If any man defile the temple of God, him shall God destroy; for the temple of God is holy, which temple ye are (I Corinthians 3:16,17).

Thou shalt come to thy grave in a full age, like as a shock of corn cometh in in his season (Job 5:26).

. . . For this purpose the Son of God was manifested, that he might destroy the works of the devil (I John 3:8).

The Blessing: Freedom from Ulcers
He healeth the broken in heart, and bindeth up their wounds (Psalms 147:3).

The Blessing: Forgiveness
And when ye stand praying, forgive, if ye have ought against any: that your Father also which is in heaven may forgive you your trespasses. But if ye do not forgive, neither will your Father which is in heaven forgive your trespasses (Mark 11:25,26).

But I say unto you, Love your enemies, bless them that curse you, do good to them that hate you, and pray for them which despitefully use you, and persecute you; That ye may be the children of your Father which is in heaven: for he maketh his sun to rise on the evil and on the good, and sendeth rain on the just and on the unjust (Matthew 5:44,45).

The Blessing: Family Salvation

And they said, Believe on the Lord Jesus Christ, and thou shalt be saved, and thy house (Acts 16:31).

Then Peter said unto them, Repent, and be baptized every one of you in the name of Jesus Christ for the remission of sins, and ye shall receive the gift of the Holy Ghost. For the promise is unto you, and to your children, and to all that are afar off, even as many as the Lord our God shall call (Acts 2:38,39).

. . . rejoice, because your names are written in heaven (Luke 10:20).

For whosoever shall call upon the name of the Lord shall be saved (Romans 10:13).

The Blessing: Loved Ones' Salvation

That if thou shalt confess with thy mouth the Lord Jesus, and shalt believe in thine heart that God hath raised him from the dead, thou shalt be saved. For with the heart man believeth unto righteousness; and with the mouth confession is made unto salvation (Romans 10:9,10).

The Blessing: Longevity

Ye shall walk in all the ways which the LORD your God hath commanded you, that ye may live, and that it may be well with you, and that ye may prolong your days in the land which ye shall possess (Deuteronomy 5:33).

The Blessing: Worthiness

For he hath made him to be sin for us, who knew no sin; that we might be made the righteousness of God in him (II Corinthians 5:21).

The Blessing: Restoration

For I will restore health unto thee, and I will heal thee of thy wounds, saith the LORD; . . . (Jeremiah 30:17).

The Blessing: Peace of Mind

Delight thyself also in the LORD; and he shall give thee the desires of thine heart (Psalms 37:4).

Casting all your care upon him; for he careth for you (I Peter 5:7).

Rejoice in the Lord alway: and again I say, Rejoice (Philippians 4:4).

Not that I speak in respect of want: for I have learned, in whatsoever state I am, therewith to be content (Philippians 4:11).

Be careful for nothing; but in everything by prayer and supplication with thanksgiving let your requests be made known unto God. And the peace of God, which passeth all understanding, shall keep your hearts and minds through Christ Jesus (Philippians 4:6,7).

ENDNOTES

1 Stokes, Burton and Lynn Lucas, <u>No Longer a Victim,</u>
(Shippensburg, PA: Destiny Image Publishers, Inc., 1988), p. 25.

2 Ibid., p. 26.

3 Ibid., pp. 27-28.

4 Ibid., p. 29.

5 Ibid., p. 31.

6 Ibid., p. 32-34.

7 Frasure, Basil, <u>How To Destroy the Evil Tree,</u> (San Angelo,
TX:Whole Person Counseling, 1994), pp. 19-22.

8 Ibid., pp. 29-30.

9 Ibid., p. 34.

10 Hickey, Marilyn, <u>I Can Be Born Again and Spirit Filled,</u>
(Denver, CO: Marilyn Hickey Ministries, 1984), pp. 34-35.

Receive Jesus Christ as Lord and Savior of Your Life.

The Bible says, *"That if thou shalt confess with thy mouth the Lord Jesus, and shalt believe in thine heart that God raised him from the dead, thou shalt be saved. For with the heart man believeth unto righteousness; and with the mouth confession is made unto salvation"* (Romans 10:9,10).

To receive Jesus Christ as Lord and Savior of your life, sincerely pray this prayer from your heart:

Dear Jesus,

I believe that You died for me and that You rose again on the third day. I confess to You that I am a sinner and that I need Your love and forgiveness. Come into my life, forgive my sins, and give me eternal life. I confess You now as my Lord. Thank You for my salvation!

Signed _____ Date _____

Please print.

Mr. & Mrs.
Mr.
Miss
Name Mrs. _____

Address _____

City _____ State _____ Zip _____

Phone(H) (   ) _____

Write to us.
We will send you information to help you
with your new life in Christ.

Marilyn Hickey Ministries
P.O. Box 17340 • Denver, CO 80217 • 303-770-0400
www.mhmin.org

Marilyn Hickey Ministries

Marilyn was a public school teacher when she met Wallace Hickey. After their marriage, Wally was called to the ministry and Marilyn began teaching home Bible studies.

The vision of Marilyn Hickey Ministries is to "cover the earth with the Word"(Isaiah 11:9). For more than 30 years, Marilyn Hickey has dedicated herself to an anointed, unique, and distinguished ministry of reaching out to people— from all walks of life—who are hungry for God's Word and all that He has for them. Millions have witnessed and acclaimed the positive, personal impact she brings through fresh revelation knowledge that God has given her through His Word.

Marilyn and Wally adopted their son Michael. Then through a fulfilled prophecy they had their daughter Sarah who, with her husband Reece Bowling, is now part of the ministry.

Marilyn has been the invited guest of government leaders and heads of state from many nations of the world. She is considered by many to be one of today's greatest ambassadors of God's Good News to this dark and hurting generation. The more Marilyn follows God's will for her life, the more God uses her to bring refreshing, renewal, and revival to the Body of Christ throughout the world. As His obedient servant, Marilyn desires to follow Him all the days of her life.

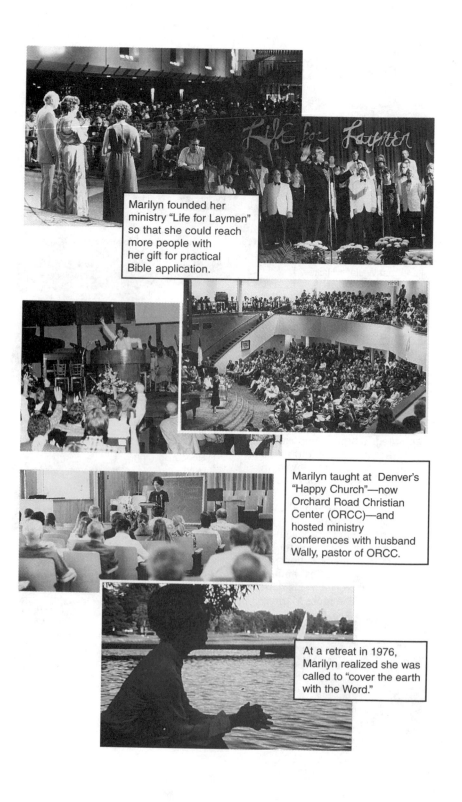

Marilyn founded her ministry "Life for Laymen" so that she could reach more people with her gift for practical Bible application.

Marilyn taught at Denver's "Happy Church"—now Orchard Road Christian Center (ORCC)—and hosted ministry conferences with husband Wally, pastor of ORCC.

At a retreat in 1976, Marilyn realized she was called to "cover the earth with the Word."

The ministry staff in the early days helped Marilyn answer the mail that came in response to her first 15-minute radio show.

Soon Marilyn realized she could reach more people through television. She and Wally hosted many well-known guests.

In Guatemala with former President Ephraim Rios-Mott

Marilyn has been the invited guest of government leaders and heads of state from many nations of the world.

In Egypt with Mrs. Anwar Sadat

In Venezuela with former first lady Mrs. Perez

Marilyn ministered to guerillas in Honduras and brought food and clothing to the wives and children who were encamped with their husbands.

The popular Bible reading plan *Time With Him* began in 1978 and invited people to "read through the Bible with Marilyn." The monthly ministry magazine has since been renamed *Outpouring*. It now includes a calendar of ministry events, timely articles, and featured product offers.

Through Word to the World College (formerly Marilyn Hickey Bible College), Marilyn is helping to equip men and women to take the gospel around the world.

Sarah Bowling taught at Riverview Christian Academy for several years before her marriage, wrote correspondence courses for the Bible college…and has since joined the ministry full-time where she combines teaching at WWC with ministry trips and Crusades.

God opened doors for the supplying of Bibles to many foreign lands—China, Israel, Poland, Ethiopia, Russia, Romania, and the Ukraine, just to name a few.

The only woman on the board of directors of Dr. Cho's Church Growth International in Korea, Marilyn has spoken at his church many times and has also been a featured speaker at the Church Growth Conference held in Japan.

An international satellite broadcast was simulcast live from Israel to U.S. cities.

Marilyn made a series of trips to African refugee camps, supplying food for feeding programs and Bibles for the famine and war-stricken communities.

Sarah began traveling overseas with her parents at an early age and developed a heart for missions.

Both Marilyn and Sarah have a strong heart for China, and have distributed thousands of Bibles and tracts there and in Russia.

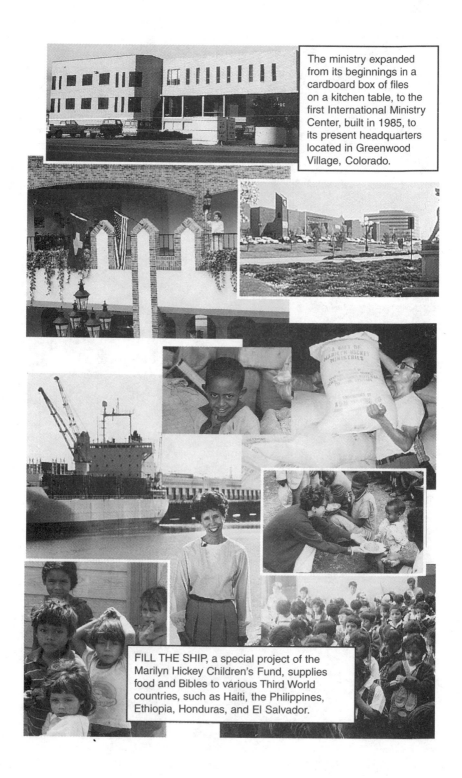

The ministry expanded from its beginnings in a cardboard box of files on a kitchen table, to the first International Ministry Center, built in 1985, to its present headquarters located in Greenwood Village, Colorado.

FILL THE SHIP, a special project of the Marilyn Hickey Children's Fund, supplies food and Bibles to various Third World countries, such as Haiti, the Philippines, Ethiopia, Honduras, and El Salvador.

The prime time television special, "A Cry for Miracles," featured co-host Gavin MacLeod.

Marilyn has been a guest several times on the 700 Club with host Pat Robertson.

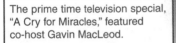

Marilyn ministered in underground churches in Romania before any of the European communist countries were officially open.

Marilyn Hickey's Prayer Center handles calls from all over the U.S.— ministering to those who need agreement in prayer.

More than 1,500 ministry products help people in all areas of their life.

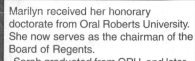

Marilyn received her honorary
doctorate from Oral Roberts University.
She now serves as the chairman of the
Board of Regents.
   Sarah graduated from ORU, and later
earned her Masters in History.

Marilyn and her Faith Covenant
Partners respond to countless
needs across the world. . .the
devastating earthquakes in Mexico
City, Romanian orphans, leprosy
victims in Africa, orphans in war-torn
Rwanda, street children in Brazil. . .
all are touched by God's power.

MHM supports Mission of Mercy in Calcutta, headed by Huldah Buntain. Marilyn has made several trips there.

Airlift Manila provided much needed food, Bibles, and personal supplies to the Philippines; MHM also raised funds to aid in the digging of water wells for those without clean drinking water.

"Today With Marilyn," featuring Marilyn and Sarah teaching the Bible, is broadcast weekdays on TBN, BET, GEB, TLN, and several independent stations. The program is also seen overseas by millions through Christian Channel Europe, in Australia on Network 10, and in more than 80 other countries worldwide.

Marilyn ministers to and teaches thousands at Miracle Healing Crusades and meetings overseas, as well as in the U.S. Sarah has joined Marilyn in this endeavor, speaking in many churches throughout the U.S. and abroad.

Exciting ministry opportunities awaited Marilyn, Sarah, and their team of travelers in the Ukraine and Russia, as the doors opened for the Gospel.

Victim of the nuclear power plant disaster in Chernobyl

Marilyn has held Bible Encounters in Malaysia and Singapore. While traveling through Hong Kong she ministered to Vietnamese in a refugee camp.

National Womens' Conferences and Pastors' Wives' Conventions were held across the U.S., exhorting women to "Change Their World!"

"Mastering Your Ministry: A Woman's Mentoring Clinic" is Marilyn's new concept for providing in-depth teaching and personal ministry in an intimate setting.

The New York area Crusade hosted well-known national ministers and ministered to thousands at the Meadowlands Arena in New Jersey.

Ministry trips and cruises to places such as Indonesia, China, Russia, Greece, the Ukraine, Turkey, Africa, and Israel offer short-term missions' opportunities to travel to exotic places and minister with Marilyn and Sarah.

MHM now operates offices in several countries. Marilyn and Sarah also host yearly meetings, Crusades, and missions' projects in those countries.

Crowds of up to 200,000 attended the open-air Crusade in Bangalore, India.

In Islamabad, Pakistan, Marilyn held Ministry Training Schools. Total Crusade attendance was estimated at 70,000.

Ministry Training Schools are held in many Third World countries, such as Sudan and Tanzania, and provide training and native language literature for local pastors and church leaders. Nightly Crusades are held to minister to the local populations.